A Christian's Secret of a

Happy Life

Hannah Whitall Smith

Publisher's Note

We offer this classic message, updated and revised, to all believers who sincerely desire to press on in their blessed walk with the Lord. Hannah Whitall Smith's originial intent has not been altered, nor has the teaching which has blessed so many. May you discover the Christian's secret of a happy life.

A CHRISTIAN'S SECRET OF A HAPPY LIFE

CONTENTS

Part III
RESULTS

PREFACE

What I have to say in this little book is not a new story. The early Church taught it in the days of the Apostles, and from those days, down to the present time voices whose lives have proclaimed it have been found in every age.

It has been lost sight of many times, and it is then that the Church has fallen into almost hopeless darkness and lifelessness. But the "secret" has always been preserved by an apostolic succession of those who have walked and talked with God.

The truth has been revived afresh in the present day, and my book is an effort to present it in a way that will be simple enough for all to understand. Too often the language of Christianity, like the repeated chimes of a bell, seems to lose the power to attract attention. It may even be that a bell of inferior tone will be able to break the careless inattention of some souls.

I have not tried to make my book theological. I have simply sought to tell the blessed story, so old and yet so new, in the familiar words of everyday life.

The truths I have to tell are practical. They are the fundamental truths of life and experience. We will find in these truths the realities of the life of salvation under the Lordship of Jesus Christ.

The book is sent out in tender sympathy and yearning love for all struggling, weary souls. Its message goes right from my heart to theirs. I have given the best I have and can do no more. I pray the Lord may use it as a voice to teach those who sorely need it, the true "secret of a happy life."

H.W.S.

Part I

THE LIFE

Chapter 1

IS IT SCRIPTURAL?

The potential for a happy abundant Christian life is available to all who would make Jesus the Lord of their lives, yet there are many Christians whose lives lack the joy and fullness of a truly happy life. A keen observer once said to me, "You Christians seem to have a religion that makes you miserable. You are like a man with a headache. He does not want to get rid of his head, but it hurts him to keep it. You cannot expect outsiders to seek earnestly for anything so uncomfortable." Then, for the first time I saw that the religion of Christ ought to be, and was meant to be, something that would make its possessors happy, not miserable. I began then and there to ask the Lord to show me the secret of a happy Christian life.

I will try to present what I have learned about this secret in the following pages. All of God's children, I am convinced, feel instinctively in their moments of divine illumination, that a life of inward rest and outward victory is their inalienable birthright. Can you not remember the shout of triumph your souls gave when you first became acquainted with the Lord Jesus, and had a glimpse of His mighty saving power? How sure you were of victory, then! How easy it seemed to be more than conquerors through Him that loved you! Under the leadership of a Captain who had never been defeated in battle, how could you dream of defeat! And yet, how different the experience has been for many of you. Your victories have been few and brief, your defeats many and disastrous. You have not lived as you feel children of God ought to live. You have had, perhaps, a clear understanding of doctrinal truths, but you have not come into possession of their life and power. You have rejoiced in your knowledge of the things revealed in the Scriptures, but have not had a living realization of the things themselves, consciously felt in the soul. Christ is believed in, talked about, and served. However, He is not known as the very life of the soul, abiding there forever, and revealing Himself there continually in His beauty.

You have found Jesus as your Savior from the penalty of sin, but you have not found Him as your Savior from its power. You have carefully studied the Holy Scriptures and have gathered much precious truth from them. You have trusted that this would feed and nourish your spiritual life. But in spite of it all, your souls are starving and dying within you. You cry out in secret, again and again, for that bread and water of life which you see promised in the Scriptures to all believers. In the very depths of your heart, you know that your experience is not a Scriptural experience. As an old writer said, your religion is "merely *talk* whereas, the early Christians enjoyed, possessed, and lived it." Your hearts have weakened within you, as day after day, and year after year, your early visions of triumph have grown dimmer. You have accepted that the best you can expect from your religion is a life of alternate failure and victory—one hour sinning and the next repenting, and then beginning again, only to fail and repent again.

But *is* this all? Did the Lord Jesus only have this in His mind when He laid down His precious life to deliver you from your bondage to sin? Did He only propose this partial deliverance? Did He intend to leave you struggling under a weary consciousness of defeat and discouragement?

When all those declarations were made concerning His coming, and the work He was to accomplish, did they only refer to a limited experience of victorious living? Was there a hidden clause in each promise that was meant to deprive it of its complete fulfillment? Did "delivered us out of the hand of our enemies" (Luke 1:74) mean that they should still have dominion over us? Did "always causeth us to triumph" (2 Corinthians 2:14) mean that we were only to triumph sometimes? Did being made "more than conquerors through Him that loved us" (Romans 8:37) mean constant defeat and failure? Does "able. . .to save them to the uttermost" (Hebrews 7:25) mean the meager salvation we see manifested among us now? Can we believe that the Savior, who was wounded for our transgressions and bruised for our iniquities, could possibly be satisfied with the many meager Christian lives in the Church today? The Bible tells us that "For this purpose the Son of God was manifested, that He might destroy the works of the devil" (1 John 3:8). Can we ever imagine that this is beyond His power, and that He finds Himself unable to accomplish the thing He was manifested to do?

Complete Deliverance From Sin

Concentrate in the very beginning on this one thing: Jesus came to save you, now, in *this* life, from the power and dominion of sin, and to make you more than conquerors through His power. If you doubt this, search your Bible and make note of every announcement or declaration concerning the purposes and object of His death on the cross. You will be astonished to find how full they are. His victory delivers us from our sins, our bondage, and our defilement. There is no scripture that supports only a limited and partial deliverance. Yet, many Christians unfortunately are satisfied with just that!

Consider some scriptural references on this subject. When the angel of the Lord appeared to Joseph in a dream and announced the coming birth of the Savior, he said, "and thou shalt call his name Jesus: for He shall save His people from their sins" (Matthew 1:21).

When Zacharias was "filled with the Holy Ghost" (Luke 1:67) at the birth of his son and "prophesied," he declared that God had visited his people in order to fulfill the promise and the oath He had made them. The promise was "That He would grant unto us, that we being delivered out of the hand of our enemies might serve Him without fear, in holiness and righteousness before Him, all the days of our life" (Luke 1:74,75).

When Peter was preaching on the porch of the temple to the wondering Jews, he said, "Unto you first God, having raised up His Son Jesus, sent Him to bless you, in turning away every one of you from his iniquities" (Acts 3:26).

When Paul was telling the Ephesian Church the wondrous truth that Christ had so loved them as to give Himself for them, he went on to declare that His purpose in doing so was "that He might sanctify and cleanse it with the washing of water by the word, that He might present it to Himself a glorious church, not having spot, or wrinkle, or any such thing; but that it should be holy and without blemish" (Ephesians 5:26,27).

When Paul was seeking to instruct Titus, his own son after the common faith, concerning the grace of God, he declared that the object of that grace was to teach us "that, denying ungodliness and worldly lusts, we should live soberly, righteously, and godly in this present world" (Titus 2:12). He adds, as the reason for this, that Christ "gave Himself for us, that He might redeem us from all iniquity, and purify unto Himself a peculiar people, zealous of good works" (Titus 2:14).

When Peter was urging Christians to be holy and

Christ-like, he told them that "even hereunto were ye called: because Christ also suffered for us, leaving us an example that ye should follow His steps: Who did no sin, neither was guile found in His mouth" (1 Peter 2:21,22). He adds, "Who His own self bare our sins in His own body on the tree, that we, being dead to sins, should live unto righteousness: by whose stripes ye were healed" (1 Peter 2:24).

In Ephesians, when Paul contrasts the walk suitable for a Christian with the walk of an unbeliever, he presents the truth in Jesus as being this, "That ye put off concerning the former conversation the old man, which is corrupt according to the deceitful lusts; and be renewed in the spirit of your mind; and that ye put on the new man, which after God is created in righteousness and true holiness" (Ephesians 4:22-24).

In the sixth chapter of Romans, Paul forever answered the question regarding a child of God who continues in sin, and showed how utterly foreign it was to the whole spirit and aim of the salvation of Jesus. He brings up our death and resurrection with Christ as an unanswerable argument for our practical deliverance from sin, and says, "God forbid. How shall we, that are dead to sin, live any longer therein? Know ye not, that so many of us as were baptized into Jesus Christ were baptized into His death? Therefore we are buried with Him by baptism into death: that like as Christ was raised up from the dead by the glory of the Father, even so we also should walk in newness of life'' (Romans 6:2-4). He adds, "Knowing this, that our old man is crucified with Him, that the body of sin might be destroyed, that henceforth we should not serve sin" (Romans 6:6).

Sin Contrary To God

In the declarations concerning the purpose of the death of Christ, far more mention is made of a present salvation from sin than of a future salvation in a heaven beyond. This plainly shows God's estimate of the relative importance of these two things.

Dear Christians, do you receive the testimony of Scripture on this matter? The same crucial questions that troubled the Church in Paul's day are troubling it now. We must consider two things. First, "Shall we continue in sin that grace may abound?" (Romans 6:1). And second, "Do we then make void the law through faith?" (Romans 3:31). Will our answer to these questions be Paul's emphatic "God forbid," and his triumphant statements that, instead of making it void, "we establish the law"? Romans 8:3-4 tells us "what the law could not do, in that it was weak through the flesh, God sending His own Son in the likeness of sinful flesh, and for sin, condemned sin in the flesh: That the righteousness of the law might be fulfilled in us, who walk not after the flesh, but after the Spirit."

Can we suppose that the holy God who hates sin in the sinner is willing to tolerate it in the Christian? Can we really believe that He has even

15

arranged the plan of salvation in such a way as to make it impossible for those who are saved from the guilt of sin to find deliverance from its power?

Dr. Chalmers says it well, "Sin is that scandal which must be rooted out from the great spiritual household over which God rejoices. . .It would indeed be strange to believe that sin, so hateful to God, caused death, and yet believe that sin should be permitted to continue. It would be very strange that what was previously the object of destroying vengeance should now become the object of toleration. Now that the penalty is removed, do you think it is possible that the unchangeable God has given up His aversion to sin so that ruined and redeemed man may now indulge, under the new arrangement, in that which under the old destroyed him? Does not the God who loved righteousness and hated iniquity six thousand years ago still love righteousness and hate iniquity?

"We can now walk before God in peace and graciousness. How can we believe that God would be allied with a persistent sinner? How will we, recover from such a catastrophe, continue that which first involved us in it? The cross of Christ, by the same mighty and decisive stroke with which it took the curse of sin away from us, also surely takes away the power and the love of sin."

Dr. Chalmers and many other holy men of his generation, and our own generation, have united in declaring that the redemption accomplished for us by our Lord Jesus Christ on the cross at Calvary is a redemption from the power of sin as well as from its guilt. Christ *is* able to save to the utter-most all who come unto God by Him.

A Quaker clergyman of the seventeenth century says: "There is nothing so contrary to God as sin, and God will not tolerate sin ruling man, His masterpiece. When we consider how God's mighty power destroys *that which is contrary to Him*, who can believe that the devil must always stand and prevail? I believe it is inconsistent with true faith for people to be Christians and yet to believe that Christ, the eternal Son of God, to whom all power in heaven and earth is given, will tolerate sin and the devil having dominion.

Power Over Sin

But you will say that no man can redeem himself by his own power, and no man can live without sin. Amen to that. But if men tell us that God's power cannot help us and redeem us out of sin, we cannot accept it!

Would you agree if I should tell you that God puts forth His power to help keep us from sinning, but the devil hinders Him? Would you believe it is impossible for God to do it, because the devil does not like it? Would you believe that it is impossible that anyone should be free from sin because the devil has such power over them that God cannot cast him out? This is not so yet hasn't this been preached? This kind of teaching says that although God's power is available, it is impossible to get rid of sin because the devil has rooted sin deeply in man's nature. Isn't man God's creature, and can't

God make man new and cast sin out of him? I do agree that sin is deeply rooted in man. Yet Christ Jesus has entered so deeply into the root of man's nature that He has received power to destroy the devil and his works, and to recover and redeem man into righteousness and holiness. Otherwise, it is not true that "He is able to save. . .to the uttermost (all) that come unto God by Him" (Hebrews 7:25). We must throw away the Bible if we say that it is impossible for God to deliver man out of sin.

When our friends are in captivity in foreign lands, we pay money for their redemption. But we would not pay our money if they were still kept in chains. One would think himself cheated to pay so much money for their redemption and make the bargain that although one be *said* to be redeemed and be *called* a redeemed captive, he must still wear his chains. This refers to bodies, but I am now speaking of souls. Christ must be my redemption and rescue me from captivity. Am I a prisoner anywhere? Yes, "Verily, verily, whosoever committeth sin, saith Christ, is the servant of sin." (John 8:34). If you have sinned, you are a slave, a captive who must be redeemed out of captivity.

You may say, "Who will pay a price for me? I am poor and have nothing. I cannot redeem myself. Who will pay a price for me?" There is One who has paid the price. What good news! He is Jesus, the Redeemer. He *will* free you from captivity.

Yet some say we must abide in sin as long as we live. What! Must we never be delivered? Must this crooked heart and perverse will always remain? Must I be a believer and yet have no faith that I can be sanctified and live a holy life? Can I never have mastery, can I never have victory over sin? Must it prevail over me as long as I live? What sort of a Redeemer then, is this, or what benefit do I have in this life of redemption?

Ask God to open the eyes of your understanding by His Spirit, that you may know, "what is the exceeding greatness of His power to usward who believe, according to the working of His mighty power, which he wrought in Christ, when He raised Him from the dead, and set Him at His own right hand in the heavenly places" (Ephesians 1:19,20). And when you have begun to have some faint glimpses of this power, learn to look completely away from your own weakness. Put your case into His hands and trust Him to deliver you.

"When thou goest out to battle against thine enemies, and seest horses, and chariots, and a people more than thou, be not afraid of them: for the Lord thy God is with thee, which brought thee up out of the land of Egypt. And it shall be, when ye are come nigh unto the battle, that the priest shall approach and speak unto the people, and shall say unto them, Hear, O Israel, ye approach this day unto battle against your enemies: let not your hearts faint, fear not, and do not tremble, neither be ye terrified because of them; for the Lord your God is He that goeth with you, to fight for you against your enemies to save you" (Deuteronomy 20:1-4).

Chapter 2

GOD'S SIDE AND MAN'S SIDE

There is much misunderstanding about the subject of the life and walk of faith because its two sides are not seen clearly. People are apt to think that there is only one side to it. They dwell exclusively upon the one they happen to see more clearly, without even thinking of any other. It is no wonder then, that there are distorted views of the whole matter.

Now, there are two very distinct sides to this subject, and like all other subjects, it cannot be fully understood unless both of these sides are kept constantly in view. I refer of course to God's side and man's side. In other words, to God's part in the work of sanctification, and man's part. These are very distinct and even contrasting, but they are not really contradictory.

At one time this was very strikingly illustrated to me. There were two preachers holding meetings in the same place at alternate hours. One spoke only of God's part in the work, and the other dwelt exclusively upon man's part. They were both in perfect sympathy with each other, and realized fully that they were each teaching different sides of the same great truth. This was also understood by a large proportion of their listeners. But some of the listeners did not comprehend this and one lady said to me in great perplexity, "I cannot understand it at all. Here are two preachers undertaking to teach just the same truth, and yet to me they seem flatly to contradict each other." I felt at the time that she expressed a puzzle that, very often, causes great difficulty in the minds of many honest inquirers after this truth.

Suppose two friends go to see a famous building and return home to describe it. One has seen only the north side, and the other only the south. The first says: "The building was built in such a manner and has so many stories and ornaments." "Oh, no," says the other, interrupting him, "you are altogether mistaken. I saw the building, and it was built in quite a different manner, and its ornaments and stories were so and so." A lively dispute might follow upon the truth of the respective descriptions, until the two friends discover that they had been describing different *sides* of the same building, and then all would be reconciled at once.

I would like to state, as clearly as I can, what I judge to be the two distinct sides in this matter. I would like to show how looking at one, without seeing the other, will be sure to create wrong impressions and views of the truth.

Man's Part In Faith

To state it briefly, I would say that man's part is to trust, and God's part is to work. It can be seen at a glance how these two parts contrast with each other, and yet are not necessarily contradictory. I mean this: there is a certain *work* to be accomplished. We are to be delivered from the power of sin, and are to be made perfect in every good work to do the will of God. "Beholding as in a glass the glory of the Lord," we are to be actually "changed into the same image from glory to glory, even as by the Spirit of the Lord" (2 Corinthians 3:18). We are to be transformed by the renewing of our minds, that we may prove what is good, acceptable, and the perfect will of God.

A real work is to be wrought in us and upon us. Sins with which we constantly struggle are to be conquered. Evil habits are to be overcome. Wrong attitudes and feelings are to be rooted out. A positive transformation is to take place. So, at least, the Bible teaches. Now, somebody must *do* this. Either we must do it for ourselves, or another must do it for us. Most of us have tried to do it for ourselves at first, and have grievously failed. We then discover, from the Scriptures and from our own experience, that it is something we are unable to do. But, the Lord Jesus Christ has come on purpose to do it. He will do it for all who put themselves into His hands and trust Him completely.

God's Part In Faith

Now, under these circumstances, what is the part of the believer, and what is the part of the Lord? Plainly the believer can do nothing but trust. The Lord, in whom he trusts, actually does the work entrusted to Him. *Trusting* and *doing* are certainly contrasted things, often indeed contradictory, but are they contradictory in this case? No, because it is two different parties that are concerned. If we should say that one party in a transaction trusted his case to another, and yet attended to it himself, we should state a contradiction and an impossibility. But, when we say that one party in a transaction trusts the other to do something, and that the other goes to work and does it, we are stating something that is perfectly simply and harmonious. When we say, therefore, that in this higher life man's part is to trust, and God's part is to do the thing entrusted to Him, we do not present a very difficult or puzzling problem.

The preacher, who is speaking on man's part in the matter, cannot speak of anything but surrender and trust, because this is positively all the man can do. We all agree about this. And yet such preachers are constantly criticized as though, in saying this, they had meant to imply there *was* no other part, and that nothing but trusting is to be done. And the cry goes out that this doctrine of faith does away with all realities. Souls are told to trust, and that is the end of it. They then sit down in a sort of religious easy-chair, dreaming away their life, fruitless of any actual result.

All this misunderstanding arises from the fact that either the preacher has neglected to state, or the hearer has failed to hear that the Lord works not by us, but by Him. Actual results are reached by our trusting, because our Lord undertakes the thing entrusted to Him and accomplishes it. *We* do not do anything, but *He* does it, and it is done all the better because of this. As soon as this is clearly seen, the difficulty disappears entirely.

On the other hand, the preacher who dwells on God's part is criticized on a totally different ground. He does not speak of trust, for the Lord's part is not trust, but to work. The Lord's part is to *do* the thing entrusted to Him. He disciplines and trains by inward exercises and outward divine care or direction. He brings to us all the refining and purifying resources of His wisdom and His love. He makes everything in our lives and circumstances subservient to the one great purpose of causing us to grow in grace, and of conforming us, day by day and hour by hour, to the image of Christ. He carries us through a process of transformation, longer or shorter as our particular case may require. And soon, we see actual results concerning what we have given Him in trust. We have dared, for instance, according to the command in Romans 6:11, to believe ourselves dead unto sin by faith. The Lord makes this a reality.

The Potter And The Clay

Sanctification is both a step of faith and a process of works. It is a step of surrender and trust on our part, and it is a process of development on God's part. By a step of faith we become members of the Body of Christ. By a process we are made to "grow up into Him in all things" (Ephesians 4:15). By a step of faith we put ourselves into the hands of the Divine Potter. By a gradual process He makes us into "a vessel unto (His own) honor, fit for (His) use and prepared unto every good work" (2 Timothy 2:21). To illustrate this, suppose I were to describe to a person, who was entirely ignorant of the subject, the way in which a lump of clay is made into a beautiful vessel. I first tell him about the role of the clay in the matter. All I can say is that the clay is put into the potter's hands and then lies passive there, submitting itself to all the turnings and overturnings of the potter's hands upon it. There is really nothing else to be said about the clay's part. If he is an intelligent listener he would say, "I understand. That *is* what the clay must do. But what must the potter do?" "Ah," I answer, "now we come to the important part. The potter takes the clay and begins to mold and fashion it according to his own will. He kneads and works it. He tears it apart and presses it together again. He wets it and then lets it dry. Sometimes he works at it for hours. Sometimes he lays it aside for days and doesn't touch it. And then, when he has made it perfectly pliable in his hands, he proceeds to make it into the vessel he has designed. He turns it upon the wheel, planes it and smooths it, dries it in the sun, bakes

25

it in the oven, and finally turns it out of his work-shop, a vessel to his honor, and fit for his use."

Before, I was speaking of the clay's part in the matter. I am now speaking of the potter's part. These two are necessarily contrasted, but are not in the least contradictory. The clay is not expected to do the potter's work. It only yields itself to his working. It seems to me that nothing could be clearer than the perfect harmony between these two *apparently* contradictory sorts of teaching.

What *can* be said about man's part in this great work is that he must continually surrender himself and continually trust. But when we come to God's side of the question, much can be said about the many wonderful ways in which He accomplishes the work entrusted to Him. It is here that growing is important. The lump of clay could never grow into a beautiful vessel if it stayed in the clay-pit for thousands of years. But when it is put into the hands of a skillful potter it grows rapidly under his fashioning into the vessel he intends it to be. In the same way the soul, abandoned to the working of the Heavenly Potter, is made into a vessel unto honor, sanctified, and meet for the Master's use.

The Maturing Process

Having, therefore, taken the step of faith by which you have put yourself completely and absolutely into His hands, you must now expect Him to begin work. His way of accomplishing that which you have entrusted to Him, may be different from your way. But He knows, and you must be

26

satisfied.

I knew a lady who had entered into this life of faith with a great outpouring of the Spirit and a wonderful flood of light and joy. She supposed, of course, this was a preparation for some great service and expected to be put forth immediately into the Lord's harvestfield. Instead of this, almost at once her husband lost all his money, and she was shut up in her own house to attend to all sorts of domestic duties with no time or strength left for any Gospel work at all. She accepted the discipline and yielded herself up as heartily to sweep, dust, bake, and sew, as she would have done to preach, pray, or write for the Lord. As a result, through this training He made her into a vessel "meet for the Master's use, and prepared unto every good work" (2 Timothy 2:21).

Another lady entered this life of faith under similar circumstances. She also expected to be sent out to do some great work, but instead, was confined with two invalid children, to nurse, humor, and amuse all day long. Unlike the first lady, this one did not accept the training. She worried, rebelled, and lost all her blessing, retreating into a sad spiritual condition. In the beginning, she understood her part of trusting but did not understand the divine process. She took herself out of the hands of the Heavenly Potter and the vessel was marred on the wheel.

I believe many a vessel has been similarly marred by not understanding these things. The maturity of a Christian experience cannot be reached in a moment. It is the result of the work of God's Holy Spirit, who, by His energizing and transforming power, causes us to "grow up into (Christ) in all things" (Ephesians 4:15). We cannot hope to reach this maturity in any other way than by yielding ourselves completely and willingly to His mighty working. However, the sanctification the Scriptures encourage, as a *present* experience upon all believers, does not consist in maturity of growth, but in purity of heart.

From the moment the lump of clay comes under the transforming hand of the potter, it is, during each day and hour of the process, just what the potter wants it to be at that hour or on that day. Therefore, it pleases him, but it is far from being the vessel he intends it to be in the future.

A little baby may be all that he or she could be or ought to be, and may perfectly please its mother. Yet it is very far from being what that mother would wish it to be when it reaches maturity.

The apple in June is a perfect apple for June. It is the best apple that June can produce. But it is very different from the apple in October, which is a perfected apple.

God's works are perfect in every stage of their growth. Man's works are never perfect until they are in every respect complete. In this life of sanctification, all we can claim is that by an act of faith we put ourselves into the hands of the Lord for Him to work in us all the good pleasure of His will. Then, by a continuous exercise of faith, keep ourselves there. This is our part in the matter. And when we do it we are truly pleasing to God. It may require years of training and discipline to mature us into a vessel that will be in all respects to His honor and fitted to every good work.

Trust Is The Foundation

Our part is the trusting. His part is to accomplish the results. When we do our part He never fails to do His. No one ever trusted in the Lord and was confounded. Do not be afraid to trust or tell others to trust. Trust is the beginning and the continuing foundation. When we trust, the Lord works, and His work is the important part of the whole matter.

This explains that apparent contradiction which puzzles so many. They say, "In one breath you tell us to do nothing but trust, and in the next you tell us to do impossible things. How can you make such statements agree?" They can be understood just as we understand the statements concerning a saw in a carpenter's shop. We say, at one moment, that the saw has sawed the log, and the next moment declare that the carpenter has done it. The saw is the instrument used. The power that uses it is the carpenter's.

And so we, yielding ourselves unto God, and our members as instruments of righteousness unto Him, find that He works in us to will and to do of His good pleasure. We can say with Paul, "I labored. . .yet not I, but the grace of God which was with me" (1 Corinthians 15:10). In the divine order, God's working depends upon our cooperation. It was said that our Lord could do no mighty work at a certain place because of the unbelief of the people. It was not that He would not. He could not. I believe we often think that God will not, when the real truth is that He cannot. The potter, however skillful, cannot make a beautiful vessel out of a lump of clay that is never put into his hands. Neither can God make out of me a vessel unto His honor, unless I put myself into His hands. My part is the essential correlation of God's part in the matter of my salvation. As God is *sure* to do His part all right, the vital thing for me is to find out what my part is, and then do it.

In this book, I will dwell mostly upon man's side. I am writing for human beings, in the hope of making it plain as to how we are to fulfill our part in this great work. But I wish it to be distinctly understood, that unless I believed with all my heart in God's effectual working on His side, not one word of this book would ever have been written.

Chapter 3

THE LIFE DEFINED

In the first chapter I have tried to settle the question regarding the scriptural basis of the experience sometimes called the higher Christian life. It is the only *true* Christian life which is best described in the words, the "life hid with Christ in God" (Colossians 3:3). In the second chapter I have sought to bring the two distinct sides of this life together—the part to be done by the Lord and the part to be done by ourselves. I will now consider the point to be settled. The Bible presents a life of abiding rest and continual victory to the believer in the Lord Jesus. That is far beyond ordinary Christian experience. The Bible presents a Savior who saves us from the power of our sins just as He saves us from the guilt of sin.

The next point to be considered concerns the nature of the chief characteristics of this "life hid with Christ in God," and how it differs from the greater part of Christian experience.

The chief characteristics of the higher Christian life are: a complete surrender to the Lord; a perfect trust in Him, resulting in victory over sin; and finally, inward rest of soul. It differs from the lower range of Christian experience in that it causes us to let the Lord carry our burdens and manage our affairs for us, instead of trying to do it ourselves.

Getting Rid Of Burdens

Most Christians are like a man who was toiling along the road, bending under a heavy burden, when a wagon overtook him, and the driver kindly offered to help him on his journey. He joyfully accepted the offer, but when seated in the wagon, continued to bend beneath his burden, which he still kept on his shoulders. "Why don't you lay down your burden?" asked the kind-hearted driver. "Oh!" replied the man, "I feel that it is almost too much to ask you to carry me, and I could not think of letting you carry my burden too." And so Christians, who have given themselves into the care and keeping of the Lord Jesus, still continue to bend beneath the weight of their burdens, and often go weary and heavy laden throughout the whole length of their journey.

When I speak of burdens, I mean *everything* that troubles us, whether they are spiritual concerns or earthly concerns. The first burden, which I believe to be the greatest burden we have to carry in life, is self. The most difficult thing we have to manage is self. Our own daily living, our feelings, our weaknesses, and temptations—these are the things that confuse us more than anything else. In getting rid of your burdens, therefore, the first one you must get rid of is yourself. You must hand yourself, and all your inward and outward experiences, over into the care and keeping of your God, and leave it there.

He made you and He understands you. He knows how to manage you. All you must do is trust Him to do it. Say to Him, "Here, Lord, I give myself to you. I have tried in every way I could think of to manage myself and to make myself what I know I ought to be, but I have always failed. Now I give it up to you. Take complete possession of me. Work in me all the good pleasure of your will. Mold and fashion me into a vessel that seems good to you. I leave myself in your hands. I believe you will, according to your promise, make me into 'a vessel unto honour, sanctified, and meet for the Master's use, and prepared unto every good work' " (2 Timothy 2:21). At this point you must rest and trust yourself continually and absolutely to Him.

Next, you must get rid of every other burden— your health, your reputation, your Christian work, your houses, your children, and your business. In short you must get rid of every inward and outward thing that concerns you.

It is generally easier for us to trust the Lord for our future than it is to trust Him for our present life. We know we are helpless regarding the future, but we feel as if the present is in our own hands and must be carried on our own shoulders. Most of us have an unconfessed idea that it is enough to ask the Lord to carry ourselves without

33

asking Him to carry our burdens, too.

Leaving Burdens With God

I knew a Christian lady who had a very heavy earthly burden. It took away her sleep and her appetite, and there was danger of her health breaking down under it. One day, when it seemed especially heavy, she noticed lying on the table near her a little tract called "Hannah's Faith." Attracted by the title, she picked it up and began to read it, little knowing, however, that it was to create a revolution in her whole experience. The story was of a poor woman who had been carried triumphantly through life of unusual sorrow. She was giving the history of her life to a kind visitor on one occasion. When she finished the visitor said, "Oh, Hannah, I do not see how you could bear so much sorrow!" "I did not bear it," was the quick reply "the Lord bore it for me." "Yes," said the visitor, "that is the right way. We must take our troubles to the Lord." "Yes," replied Hannah, "but we must do more than that. We must *leave* them there. Most people," she continued, "take their burdens to Him, but they bring them away with them again, and are just as worried and unhappy as ever. But I take mine and leave them with Him, and come away and forget them. If the worry comes back, I take it to Him again. I do this over and over, until at last I just forget I have any worries and am at perfect rest."

My friend, very much struck with this plan, resolved to try it. She couldn't change the circumstances of her life, but she took them to the Lord and handed them over into His management. She believed that He took them, and she left all the responsibility and the worry and anxiety with Him. When the anxieties returned, she took them back to the Lord. The result was, that although the circumstances remained unchanged, her soul was kept in perfect peace in the midst of them. She felt that she had found out a practical secret. From that time she never attempted to carry her own burdens or to manage her own affairs, but to hand them over to the Lord as fast as they arose.

This same secret so effective in her outward life, also proved to be still more effective in her inward life. She gave her whole self to the Lord—with all that she was and all that she had. Believing that He took all she had committed to Him, she stopped worrying and her life changed for the better. She found out a simple secret. It was possible to obey God's commandment contained in the words, "Be careful for nothing; but in everything by prayer and supplication with thanksgiving let your requests be made known unto God" (Philippians 4:6). By obeying this promise the result would inevitably be the "peace of God, which passeth all understanding, shall keep your hearts and minds through Christ Jesus" (Philippians 4:7).

Rest In The Lord

There are many other things to be said about this life hid with Christ in God. There are many details concerning what the Lord Jesus does for those who

35

give themselves to Him. The heart of the whole matter is stated here. The soul that has discovered this secret of simple faith has found the key that will unlock the whole treasure house of God.

I am sure these pages will fall into the hands of some child of God who is hungering for such a life as I have been describing. You long unspeakably to get rid of your weary burdens. You would be delighted to hand over the management of your unmanageable self into the hands of one who is able to manage you. You are tired and weary, and what I speak about looks unutterably sweet to you.

Do you recall going to bed with a great sense of rest after a day of great exertion and weariness? How good it felt to relax every muscle and let your body go in perfect abandon of ease and comfort! The strain of the day had ceased, for a few hours at least, and the work of the day had been forgotten. You no longer had to hold up an aching head or a weary back. You trusted yourself to the bed in absolute confidence, and it held you up without effort or strain or thought on your part. You rested!

But suppose you had doubted the strength or the stability of your bed. Suppose you were frightened that at any moment it would give way beneath you and you would land on the floor. Could you have rested then? Every muscle would have been strained in a fruitless effort to hold yourself up and the weariness would be greater than if you had not gone to bed at all.

Let this analogy teach you what it means to rest in the Lord. Let your souls lie down upon the couch of His sweet will as your bodies lie down in their beds at night. Relax every strain and release every burden. Let yourself go in perfect abandon of ease and comfort. Be assured that since He holds you up you are perfectly safe. Your part is simply to rest. His part is to sustain you. He cannot fail.

Freedom From Care

Let us look at another analogy which our Lord Himself has abundantly approved—that of the child-life. For "Jesus called a little child unto Him, and set him in the midst of them, and said. . .Except ye be converted and become as little children, ye shall not enter into the kingdom of heaven" (Matthew 18:2-3).

Now, what are the characteristics of a little child, and how does it live? It lives by faith. Its chief characteristic is freedom from care. Its life is one long trust from year's end to year's end. It trusts its parents. It trusts its teacher. It even sometimes trusts people who are completely unworthy of trust. A child's trust is answered abundantly. The child provides nothing for itself and yet everything is provided. It takes no thought for the morrow, and forms no plans, and yet all its life is planned out for it. It finds its paths made ready and prepared as it comes to them day by day and hour by hour. It goes in and out of its father's house with ease. It enjoys all the good things of the home without having spent a penny in procuring them. Under its father's tender care the child does not worry about disease. Famine and fire and war may rage, but the child abides in utter unconcern and perfect rest. It lives in the present moment and receives its life unquestioningly as it comes to it day by day from its father's hands.

I was visiting once in a wealthy home where there was a little adopted child who received all the love and tenderness and care that human hearts could give. As I watched that child running in and out day by day, free and light-hearted, with the happy carelessness of childhood, I thought what a picture it was of our wonderful position as children in the house of our Heavenly Father. And I said to myself, "If the loving hearts around this child would be grieved to see her worried or anxious about herself in any way—about whether her food and clothes would be provided, or how she was to get her education or her future support. How much more must the great, loving heart of our God and Father be grieved and wounded at seeing His children taking so much anxious care and thought!" And I understood why it was that our Lord had said to us so emphatically, "Take no thought for your life" (Matthew 6:25).

Who is taken care of the best in every household? Is it not the little children? And does not the least of all, the helpless baby, receive the largest share? We all know that the baby doesn't work or sew, yet it is fed, clothed, loved, and rejoiced in more tenderly than the hardest worker of all.

This life of faith, then, about which I am writing, consists in just this—being a child in the

Father's house. And when this is said, enough is said to change every weary, burdened life into one of blessedness and rest.

Let the ways of childish confidence and freedom from care, which so please you and win your hearts in your own little ones, teach you what should be your ways with God. Leave yourselves in His hands. Learn to be literally "careful for nothing" and you will find it to be a fact that "Thou wilt keep him in perfect peace, whose mind is stayed on Thee: because he trusteth in Thee" (Isaiah 26:3).

This is is the divine description of the life of faith about which I am writing. It is no speculative theory, neither is it a dream of romance. There is such a thing as having one's soul kept in perfect peace here in this life. Child-like trust in God is the key to its attainment.

Chapter 4

HOW TO ENTER IN

Having sought to settle the question regarding the scriptural basis of actually living a life hid with Christ in God, and having also shown a little of what it is, the next point concerns how it is to be reached and realized.

First of all, I would say that this blessed life must not in any way be looked upon as an attainment, but as an obtainment. We cannot earn it. We cannot strive for it. We cannot win it. We can do nothing but ask for it and receive it. It is the gift of God in Christ Jesus. And when something is a gift, the only course left for the receiver is to take it and thank the giver for it. We never say of a gift, "See what I have attained," and boast of our skill and wisdom in having attained it. Rather we say, "See what has been given to me," and boast of the love and wealth and generosity of the giver. Everything in our salvation is a gift. From beginning to end, God is the giver and we are the receivers. God does not give to those who do great things. He gives to those who "receive abundance of grace and of the gift of righteousness'' (Romans 5:17), the richest promises.

In order to enter into a practical experience of this interior life, the soul must be in a receptive attitude, fully recognizing the fact that the higher Christian life is God's gift in Christ Jesus, and that it cannot be gained by any efforts or works of our own. This will greatly simplify the matter. The only thing left to be considered is to discover who receives this gift from God and how they receive it. In short, He can bestow it only upon the fully consecrated soul. And finally, it is to be received by faith.

Entire Surrender To God

Consecration (the act of setting apart for the service of God) removes the difficulties out of the way and makes it possible for God to bestow the higher Christian life. In order for a lump of clay to be made into a beautiful vessel, it must be entirely abandoned to the potter. It must lie passive in his hands.

I was once trying to explain to a physician who was in charge of a large hospital, the necessity and meaning of consecration, but he seemed unable to understand. At last I said to him, "Suppose, in making your rounds among your patients, you would meet with one man who earnestly asked you to take his case in your care in order to cure him, but who at the same time refused to tell you all his symptoms or to take all your prescribed remedies. Suppose he should say to you, 'I am quite willing to follow your directions regarding certain things because they seem good to me, but I prefer judging other matters for myself, and following my own directions.' What would you do in such a case?" I asked. "Do!" he replied with indignation: "Do! I would soon leave a man like that to his own care. For, of course," he added, "I could do nothing for him unless he would put his whole case into my hands without any reservations and would obey my directions implicitly." "It is necessary, then," I said, "for doctors to be obeyed, if they are to have any chance to cure their patient?" *"Implicitly obeyed!"* he replied emphatically. "And that is consecration," I continued. "God must have the whole case put into His hands without any reservations, and His directions must be implicitly followed." "I see it," he exclaimed. "I see it! And I will do it. God will have His own way with me from now on."

To some minds the word "abandonment" might express this idea better than the word "consecration." But whatever word we use, we mean an entire surrender of the whole being to God— spirit, soul, and body placed under His absolute control, for Him to do with us just what He pleases. The language of our hearts, under all circumstances and in view of every act, is to be "Thy will be done." Freedom of choice must be given up. A life of complete obedience is the key.

This may appear to be difficult to those who truly do not know God. But to those who know Him, it is the happiest and most restful of lives. He is our Father, He loves us, and He knows just what is best for us. Therefore, His will is the most blessed thing that can come to us under any circumstances. I do not understand how it is that the eyes of so many Christians have been blinded to this fact. But it really would seem as if God's own children were more afraid of His will than of anything else in life—His lovely, loveable will, which only means loving-kindnesses and tender mercies and blessings unspeakable to their souls! I wish I could show every one the immeasurable sweetness of the will of God. Heaven is a place of infinite bliss because His will is done there perfectly.

Our lives share in this bliss in the proportion that His will is perfectly done in them. He loves us—*loves us*, I say—and the will of love is always blessing for its loved one. Some of us know what it is to love, and we know that if we could only have our way, our loved ones would be overwhelmed with blessings. All that is good and sweet and lovely in life would be poured out upon them from our lavish hands, if we only had the power to carry out our will for them. And if this is the way we love, how much more it must be so with God, who is love itself! If we for one moment could get a glimpse into the mighty depths of His love, our hearts would spring out to meet His will and embrace it as our richest treasure. We would abandon ourselves to it with an enthusiasm of gratitude and joy that such a wondrous privilege could be ours.

Many Christians seem to think that all their Father in heaven wants is a chance to make them miserable and to take away all their blessings. They imagine, poor souls, that if they try to govern things by their will they can hinder Him from doing this. I am ashamed to write this, yet we must face a fact which is making hundreds of lives miserable.

A Christian who was in a great deal of trouble was telling another Christian about the various efforts he had tried for deliverance, and concluded by saying, "But it has all been in vain, and there is literally nothing left for me to do now but to trust the Lord."

"Alas!" exclaimed his friend in a tone of the deepest commiseration, as though no greater risk were possible—"Has it come to *that?*"

A Christian lady who had this feeling was once telling a friend how she found it impossible to say, "Thy will be done," and how afraid she was to do it. She was the mother of an only little boy who was the heir to a great fortune and the idol of her heart. After she had completely stated her difficulties, her friend said, "Suppose your little Charley should come running to you tomorrow and say 'Mother, I have made up my mind to let you have your own way with me from now on. I am always going to obey you, and I want you to do just whatever you think best with me. I will trust your love.' How would you feel towards him? Would you say to yourself, 'Ah, now I will have a chance to make Charley miserable. I will take away all his pleasures, and fill his life with every hard and disagreeable thing that I can find. I will compel him to do just the things that are the most difficult for him to do, and will give him all sorts of impossible commands'?" "Oh, no, no, no!" exclaimed the indignant mother. "You know I wouldn't do that. You know I would hug him to my heart, cover him with kisses, and hurry to fill his life with all that was sweetest and best." "And are you more tender and more loving than God?" asked her friend. "No!" was the reply. "I see my mistake. Of course I must not be anymore afraid of saying, 'Thy will be done,' to my Heavenly Father, than I would want my Charley to be afraid of saying it to me."

Better and sweeter than health, or friends, or money, or fame, or ease, or prosperity, is the adorable will of our God. It gilds the darkest hours with a divine halo, and sheds brightest sunshine on the gloomiest paths. When one reigns in the Kingdom, nothing can go wrong for him. Surely, then, it is only a glorious privilege that is opening before you, when I tell you that the first step you must take in order to enter into the life hid with Christ in God, is that of entire consecration. I beg you not to look at it as a difficult and stern demand. You must do it gladly, thankfully, enthusiastically. You must go in on what I call the privilege side of consecration. I can assure you, from the universal testimony of all who have tried it, that you will find it the happiest place you have ever entered yet.

45

According To Our Faith

After surrender, faith is important next. Faith is an absolutely necessary element when receiving any gift. When our friends give a thing to us, it is not really ours until we believe it has been given and we claim it as our own. Above all, this is true about gifts which are purely mental or spiritual. Love may be lavished upon us by another without measure, but until we believe that we are loved, it never really becomes ours.

I suppose most Christians understand this principle in reference to the matter of their forgiveness. They know that the forgiveness of sins through Jesus could have been preached to them forever, but it would never really have become theirs until they believed this preaching, and claimed the forgiveness as their own. But when it comes to living the Christian life, they lose sight of this principle, and think that, having been saved by faith, they are now to live by works and efforts. Instead of continuing to *receive*, they are now to begin to *do*. Our declaration that the life hid with Christ in God is to be entered by faith, seems perfectly unintelligible to them. And yet it is plainly declared, "as ye have therefore received Christ Jesus the Lord, so walk ye in Him" (Colossians 2:6). We received Him by faith, and by faith alone. Therefore, we are to walk in Him by faith, and by faith alone. And the faith by which we enter into this hidden life is the same as the faith by which we were translated out of the kingdom of darkness into the Kingdom of God's dear Son, only it lays hold of a different thing.

Then we believed that Jesus was our Savior from the guilt of sin, and according to our faith it was done for us. Now we must believe that He is our Savior from the power of sin, and according to our faith it shall be done for us. Then we trusted Him for forgiveness, and it became ours. Now we must trust Him for righteousness, and it shall become ours also. Then we took Him as Savior from the penalties of our sins in the future. Now we must take Him as a Savior in the present from the bondage of our sins. Then He was our Redeemer. Now He is to be our Life. Then He lifted us out of the pit. Now He is to seat us in heavenly places with Himself.

Theologically I know that every believer has everything as soon as he is converted. But nothing is his until he claims it by faith. "Every place that the sole of your foot shall tread upon, that have I given unto you" (Joshua 1:3). God "hath blessed us with all spiritual blessings in heavenly places in Christ" (Ephesians 1:3). But until we set the foot of faith upon them, they do not practically become ours. "According to our faith" is always the limit and the rule (see Matthew 9:29).

But this faith that I am speaking of must be a present faith. No faith that is practiced in the future tense amounts to anything. A man may believe forever that his sins will be forgiven at some future time and he will never find peace. He has to come to the *now* belief, and say by a present

47

appropriating faith, "My sins are now forgiven," before his soul can be at rest. And, similarly, no faith that looks for a future deliverance from the power of sin will ever lead a soul into the life we are describing. The enemy delights in this future faith, for he knows it is powerless to accomplish any practical results. However, he trembles and flees when the soul of the believer dares to claim a present deliverance and to consider itself to be free from his power now.

Perhaps no four words in the language have more meaning in them than the following, which I would have you repeat over and over with your voice and with your soul, emphasizing a different word each time:

Believe God Will Do It

Jesus saves me now.—It is He.

Jesus *saves* me now.—It is His work to save.

Jesus saves *me* now.—I am the one to be saved.

Jesus saves me *now*.—He is doing it every moment.

Let us sum this up. In order to enter into this blessed interior life of rest and triumph, you have two steps to take: first, entire abandonment, and second, absolute faith. No matter what the complications of your experience, no matter what your difficulties, or your surroundings, or your "peculiar temperament," these two steps will certainly bring you out into the green pastures and still waters of this life hid with Christ in God. You may be perfectly sure of this. And if you will let every other consideration go, and simply devote your attention to these two points, your progress will be rapid, and your soul will reach its desired haven far sooner than you can now think possible.

I will repeat the steps so there is no mistake. You are a child of God, and long to please Him. You love your divine Master, and you are sick and weary of the sin that grieves Him. You long to be delivered from its power. Everything you have tried up to now has failed to deliver you. Now in your despair, you are asking if it can be as happy people say, that Jesus is able and willing to deliver you. Surely you must know in your very soul that to save you out of the hand of all your enemies is, in fact, just the very thing He came to do. Then trust Him. Commit your case to Him without hesitation. Believe that He takes all. And at once, knowing what He is and what He has said, claim that He saves you even now. Just as you first believed that He delivered you from the guilt of sin because He said it, believe now that He delivers you from the power of sin because He says it.

Let your faith lay hold of a new power in Christ now. You have trusted Him as your dying Savior. Trust Him now as your living Savior. Just as He came to deliver you from future punishment, He also came to deliver you from present bondage. Just as sure as He came to bear your stripes for you, He has come to live your life for you. You are as completely powerless in the one case as in the other. You could not have gotten rid of your own sins and you could not accomplish practical righteousness for yourself. Christ, and Christ only, must do both for you. Your part in both cases is simply to give Him the thing to do, and then believe that He does it.

A woman, now very strong in this life of trust was at first in great darkness and perplexity when trying to come to an understanding of the higher Christian life. At that time she said to the friend who was trying to help her, "You all say abandon yourself and trust, abandon yourself and trust. But I don't know how. I wish you would just do it out loud, so that I can see how you do it."

Would you like me to do it out loud for you?

"Lord Jesus, I believe that you are able and willing to deliver me from all the care and unrest and bondage of my life. I believe you died to set me free, not only in the future, but here and now. I believe you are stronger than sin, and that you can keep me, even in my extreme weakness, from falling into its snares or obeying its commands. And, Lord, I am going to trust you to keep me. I have tried keeping myself, and have failed terribly. I am absolutely helpless. So now I will trust you. I give myself to you. Body, soul, and spirit, I present myself to you, as a piece of clay, to be fashioned into anything your love and your wisdom chooses. I hold back nothing. And now I *am* yours. I believe you accept all that I present to you. I believe that you have taken possession of this poor, weak, foolish heart. I believe that at this very moment you have begun to work in me to will and to do of your good pleasure. I trust you completely and I trust you now."

Are you afraid to take this step? Does it seem too sudden, too much like a leap in the dark? Don't you know that the step of faith always seems to be void, but the rock is always beneath: If you are ever to enter this glorious land flowing with milk and honey, you must first enter the brimming waters, for there is no other path. To do it now may save you months and even years of disappointment and grief. Hear the word of the Lord: "Have not I commanded thee? Be strong and of a good courage; be not afraid, neither be thou dismayed: for the Lord thy God is with thee whithersoever thou goest" (Joshua 1:9).

Part II

DIFFICULTIES

Chapter 5

DIFFICULTIES CONCERNING
CONSECRATION

It is very important that Christians not be ignorant of the temptations that seem to stand ready to oppose every step of their progress. These temptations are especially active when the soul hungers and thirsts after righteousness and begins to reach out after the fullness of life in Christ.

One of the greatest of these temptations concerns consecration. One who desires holiness is told that he must consecrate himself and he strives to do so. But he meets with difficulty at once. He has done what he thinks is necessary to be consecrated, yet he finds nothing different in his experience. Nothing seems changed as he has been led to expect it would be. He is completely baffled and desperately asks the question, "How am I to know when I am consecrated?"

The chief temptation that assaults the soul at this point and at every step of its progress concerns feelings. We can't believe we are consecrated until we feel that we are. And because we don't feel that God has taken charge of us, we can't really believe that He has. As usual, we put feeling first, faith second, and His promise last of all. Now, God's rule in everything is, His promise (His Word) first, faith second, and feeling last of all. We cannot change this order.

Put Faith Before Feeling

The way to meet this temptation concerning concentration is simply to take God's side in the matter. We must follow His way by putting faith before feeling. Give yourself completely to the Lord. Ask the Holy Spirit to show you all that is not of Him in your heart and life. If the Holy Spirit reveals anything to you, give it to the Lord immediately, and say "Thy will be done." If the Holy Spirit reveals nothing to you, you must believe that there is nothing, and must conclude that you have given Him all. Then, recognize the fact that when you give yourself to God He accepts you. Let your faith take hold of this fact at once. Firmly believe that He has taken all that you have surrendered to Him. You must not wait to feel that you have given yourself, or that God has taken you. You must simply believe it to be the case. If you are steadfast in believing, you will realize it is a blessed fact that you are completely the Lord's.

If you were to give an estate to a friend, you would have to give it, and he would have to receive it by faith. An estate is not a thing that can be picked up and handed over to another. The giving of it and the receiving of it must be a transaction of word and paper and, therefore, one of faith. Now, suppose you give an estate one day to a friend, and then doubt whether you had really given it, and whether he had actually taken it and considered it his own. Suppose you feel it necessary to go day after day and renew the gift. What would your friend think? What would be the condition of your own mind concerning it? Your friend would certainly begin to doubt whether you ever intended to give it to him at all. You yourself would be so confused about it, that you would not know whether the estate was yours or his.

Now, isn't this the same way you have been acting toward God concerning consecration? You have daily given yourself to Him over and over, perhaps for months, but you still wonder whether you really gave yourself to Him and whether He has taken you. Because you felt no change, you have concluded that it is not done. This confusion will last forever, unless you stop it by putting faith to work. You must get to the point of believing the matter to be an accomplished and settled thing.

The Levitical law of offerings to the Lord clearly states that everything which is given to Him becomes, by the very act of giving, something holy. Set apart from all other things, it is something that cannot be put to any other uses, unless sacrilege is committed. ''Notwithstanding no devoted thing, that a man shall devote unto the Lord of all that he hath, both of man and beast, and of the field of his possession, shall be sold or redeemed: every devoted thing is most holy unto the Lord" (Leviticus 27:28). Having given it once to the Lord, the devoted thing from that time on was believed by all Israel as being the Lord's. No one dared to retake it.

The giver might have grudgingly and halfheartedly made his offering, but, having made the offer, the matter was taken out of his hands altogether. The devoted thing, by God's own law, became "most holy unto the Lord." It was not made holy by the state of mind of the giver, but by the holiness of the divine receiver. "The altar sanctifieth the gift" (Matthew 23:19). An offering, once laid upon the altar, belonged to the Lord from that very moment. I can imagine someone offering a gift and then begin to question his sincerity and honesty in doing it. I can imagine his coming back to the priest to say that he was afraid because he did not give it correctly or was not perfectly sincere in giving it. I feel sure the priest would have silenced him at once, saying, "I don't know how you gave your offering, or what your motives were in giving it. The facts are that you did give it, and that it's the Lord's. For every devoted thing is most holy unto Him. It's too late to change the transaction now." Not only the priest, but all Israel, would have been aghast at the man, who, having once given his offering, would reach out his hand to take it back. Yet, day after day, sincere Christians, with no thought of the sacrilege they are committing, are guilty of a similar act. They give themselves to the Lord in solemn consecration, and then through unbelief, take back that which they have given.

Believing Brings Assurance

Because God is not visibly present to the eye, it is difficult to feel that a transaction with Him is real. If we could actually see Him when we made our acts of consecration we would feel it to be a very real thing. We would realize that we had given our word to Him and could not dare to take it back, no matter how much we might wish to do so. Such a transaction would have the same power for us as a spoken promise to an earthly friend always has to a man of honor. We need to see that God's presence is always a fact. We need to see that every act of our soul is done before Him. A word spoken in prayer is spoken to Him just as if our eyes could see Him and our hands could touch Him. We will then stop having such vague conceptions of our relations with Him and will feel the binding force of every word we say in His presence.

I know some will say, "Ah, yes. But if He would only speak to me and say that He took me when I gave myself to Him, I would have no trouble then in believing it." No, of course you wouldn't. But then, where would the room for faith be? Sight is not faith. Hearing is not faith. Neither is feeling faith. But believing when we can neither see, hear, nor feel, *is* faith. The Bible tells us our salvation is to be by faith. Therefore, we must believe before we feel, often against our feelings, if we would honor God by our faith. He who believes has assurance. He who doubts does not. But how can we doubt since His very command tells us to present ourselves a living sacrifice to Him. He has pledged to receive us.

I cannot picture an honorable man asking another to give him something which he was doubtful of taking. Still less can I picture a loving parent acting that way toward a beloved child. "My son, give me thine heart" (Proverbs 23:26), is an assurance for knowing that the moment the heart is given it will be taken by the Heavenly Father. We must be totally confident when we surrender ourselves to the Lord according to His own command. He receives us then and there, and from that moment we are His. A real transaction has taken place. It cannot be violated without dishonor on our part, and we know it will not be violated by Him.

In Deuteronomy 26:17-19 we see God's way of working under these circumstances. "Thou hast avouched the Lord this day to be thy God, and to walk in His ways, and to keep His statutes, and His commandments, and His judgments, and to hearken unto His voice: And the Lord hath avouched thee this day to be His peculiar people, as He hath promised thee, and that thou shouldest keep all His commandments. . .and that thou mayest be an holy people unto the Lord thy God, as He hath spoken."

When we confess the Lord to be our God, and express the desire to walk in His ways and keep

His commandments, He affirms that we are His, and that we *shall* keep all His commandments. And from that moment He takes possession of us. This always has been and continues to be His principle of working. "Every devoted thing is most holy to the Lord." This is stated clearly. There should be no question about it!

According To His Will

However, if you need further assurance of this, let me refer you to a New Testament verse which approaches the subject from a different angle, but which also definitely settles it. It is in 1 John 5:14,15, and reads, "And this is the confidence that we have in Him, that, if we ask anything according to His will, He heareth us: And if we know that He hears us, whatsoever we ask, we know that we *have* the petitions that we desired of Him." Is it according to His will that you should be entirely surrendered to Him? There is only one answer to this—He has *commanded* it! Is it not also according to His will that He should work in you to will and to do of His good pleasure? This question also can have only one answer, for He has declared it to be His purpose.

You know, then, that these things are according to His will. Therefore, God's own Word tells you that He hears you. Knowing this much, you are motivated to go farther and *know* that you have the petitions that you have desired of Him. That you *have*, I say, not that you will have, or may have, but have now in actual possession. It is thus that we "obtain promises" by faith. It is thus that we have "access by faith" into the grace that is given us in our Lord Jesus Christ. It is thus, and thus only, that we come to know our hearts "purified by faith," and are enabled to live by faith, to stand by faith, to walk by faith.

I wish to make this subject so clear and practical that no one need be confused about it again. I will again repeat exactly what must be done to get rid of your confusion about consecration.

I suppose that you have trusted the Lord Jesus for the forgiveness of your sins. I suppose you know something of what it means to belong to the family of God and to be made an heir of God through faith in Christ. And now you feel springing up in your heart the longing to be conformed to the image of your Lord. In order for this to happen, you must surrender yourself entirely to Him so that He may work in you all the good pleasure of His will. You have tried over and over to do it, but up to now you have not been successful. It is at this point that I desire to help you.

What you must do now is to come to Him once more in a surrender of your whole self to His will, as completely as you know how. You must ask Him to reveal to you, by His Spirit, any hidden rebellion. And if He reveals nothing, then you must believe that there *is* nothing, and that the surrender is complete. This must then be considered a settled matter. You have totally yielded yourself to the Lord, and from now on you do not in any way belong to yourself. You must never even so much as listen to a suggestion to the contrary. If you are tempted to doubt whether you really have completely surrendered yourself, face it with the assurance that you have. Don't even debate the matter. Get rid of any such idea instantly. Get rid of it firmly. You meant it then and you mean it now. You have really done it. Your emotions may question the surrender, but your will must hold firm. It is your purpose God looks at, not your feelings about that purpose. And your purpose, or will, is therefore the only thing you need to consider.

God Works In You

Once the surrender has been made, it never needs to be questioned. The next point is to believe that God takes what you have surrendered and accepts it as His. He does not accept it at some future time. He accepts it at that moment. From that point on He will begin to work in you to will and to do of His good pleasure. It is in this that you must be content. There is nothing more for you to do, except to be an obedient child. For you are the Lord's. You are entirely in His hands, and He has taken over the complete care and management and forming of you. He will, according to His word, work "in you that which is well pleasing in His sight through Jesus Christ" (Hebrews 13:21). But you must be firmly resolved here. If you begin to question your surrender, or God's acceptance of it, then your wavering faith will produce a wavering experience, and He cannot work in you to do His will. But while you trust, He works. And the result of His working is always to change you into the image of Christ by His mighty Spirit.

Do you completely surrender yourself to Him at this moment? If you answer "yes," begin at once to believe that you are His, that He has taken you, and that He is working in you to will and to do of His good pleasure. Keep on believing this. You will find it a great help to put your reckoning into words, and say over and over to yourself and to your God, "Lord, I am Yours. I give myself entirely to You. I believe that You take me. I leave myself with You. Work in me all the good pleasure of Your will, and I will only lie still in Your hands and trust You."

Make this a daily, definite act of your will, and many times a day remember it as your continual attitude before the Lord. Confess it to yourself. Confess it to your God. Confess it to your friends. Continually confess the Lord to be your God. Declare your purpose of walking in His ways and keeping His statutes. And sooner or later, you will find in practical experiece that He has taken you to be one of His peculiar people, enabling you to keep all His commandments and assuring you that you are being made into "an holy people unto the Lord, as He hath spoken" (Deuteronomy 7:6).

Chapter 6

DIFFICULTIES CONCERNING FAITH

After consecration, the next step in the soul's progress out of the wilderness of a failing Christian experience into the land that flows with milk and honey, is that of faith. And here, as in the first step, the soul encounters certain kinds of difficulty and hindrance at once.

The child of God who understands the fullness of life available to him through Jesus Christ, and whose heart hungers to experience that fullness, can be assured that this fullness is only to be received by faith. But the subject of faith is such a hopeless mystery to his mind, that the idea of faith, instead of shedding light upon the way to fullness of life in Christ, only seems to make it more difficult and involved than ever.

"Of course it must by faith," he says, "for I know that everything in the Christian life is by faith. But that is just what makes it so hard, for I have no faith, and I do not even know what it is, nor how to get it." And, thus, confused at the very beginning by this difficulty, he is plunged into darkness, and almost despair. This trouble arises from the fact that the subject of faith is very generally misunderstood. For, in reality, faith is the simplest and plainest thing in the world, and it is most easy to put into practice.

Your idea of faith, I suppose, has been something like this. You have looked upon it as a sort of *thing*—either a Christian exercise of soul, or an inward attitude of heart. You suppose it to be something tangible. In fact, when you have secured it, you suppose you can look at it and rejoice over it. You suppose you can use it as a passport to God's favor, or a coin with which to purchase His gifts. You have been praying for faith, expecting all the while to get something like this. You have never received any such thing, so now you are insisting that you have no faith.

The Simplicity Of Faith

Faith is not in the least like this. It cannot be touched. It is simply believing God. Like sight, it is nothing apart from its object. You might as well shut your eyes and look inside, and see whether you have sight, as to look inside to discover whether you have faith. You see something and know that you have sight. You believe something and know that you have faith. For as sight is only seeing, so faith is only believing. As the only necessary thing about sight is that you see the thing as it is, so the only necessary thing about belief is that you believe the thing as it is. The virtue does not lie in your believing, but in the thing you believe. If you believe the truth, you are saved. If you believe a lie, you are lost. In both cases the act of believing is the same. The things believed are exactly opposite, and it is this which makes the mighty difference. Your salvation does not come because your faith saves you. Your salvation comes because it links you to the Savior who saves. Your believing is really nothing but the link.

I beg you to recognize the extreme simplicity of faith. I beg you to recognize that it is nothing more nor less than just believing God when He says He either has done something for us, or will do it. Then trust Him to keep His word. It is so simple that it is hard to explain.

If any one asks me what it means to trust someone to do a piece of work for me, I can only answer that it means committing the work to the someone and leaving it in his hands without any feelings of anxiety. All of us trust important matters to others in this way. We feel calm in trusting because of the confidence we have in those who take care of the important matters for us. How mothers trust their precious infants to the care of nurses and feel no shadow of anxiety! How often we trust our health and our lives, without a thought of fear, to cooks and taxi drivers, and all sorts of paid workers who have us completely at their mercy. They could, if they chose to do so, or even if they failed in being careful, plunge us into misery or death in a moment. We do this and make no complaint about it. We often put our trust in people we hardly know. We require only a general knowledge of human nature as the foundation of our trust. And, we never feel as if we were doing anything in the least remarkable!

You have done this and continue to do this yourself. You could not live among your fellow-men and go through the customary routine of life for a single day, if you were unable to trust them. It never enters into your head to say you cannot live among them. Yet, you do not hesitate to continually say that you cannot trust your God! You excuse yourself by saying that you are "a poor weak creature" and "have no faith."

I wish you would try to imagine yourself acting in your human relations as you do in your spiritual relations. Suppose you should begin tomorrow with the notion that you could not trust anybody, because you had no faith. When you sat down to breakfast you would say, "I can't eat anything on this table, for I have no faith, and I can't believe the cook hasn't put poison in the coffee, or that the butcher hasn't sent home diseased or unhealthy meat." So you would starve. When you went about your daily business you would say, "I can't ride in this train because I have no faith. I can't trust the engineer, nor the conductor, nor the men who built the train, nor the men who repair the rails." You would have to walk everywhere, and would become completely exhausted. You would be unable to reach the places you could have reached in the train.

When your friends met you with any statements, or your business agent with any accounts, you would say, "I'm sorry that I can't believe you, but I have no faith, and never can believe anybody." If you opened a newspaper, you would be forced to put it down again, saying, "I really can't believe a word this paper says, for I have no faith. I don't believe there is any such person as the Queen, for I never saw her. I can't believe there is any such country as Ireland, for I was never there. I have no faith, so of course I can't believe anything that I haven't actually felt and touched myself. It's a great ordeal, but I can't help it, for I have no faith."

Just picture a day like this and see how disastrous it would be to yourself. It would be completely ridiculous to anyone who observes you. Realize how your friends would feel insulted, and how people would refuse to serve you another day. Then realize that if this lack of faith in your fellow-men would be so dreadful, what must it be when you tell God that you have no power to trust Him or to believe His word. If your friends would be insulted, imagine telling God that it is a great ordeal, but you cannot help it, "for you have no faith."

Have Confidence In The Holy Spirit

Is it possible that you can trust your fellow-men, and cannot trust your God? Is it possible that you can receive the "witness of men," and cannot receive the "witness of God?" Is it possible that you can believe man's records, and cannot believe God's record? You can commit your dearest earthly interest to your weak, failing fellow-creatures without a fear. Yet, you are afraid to commit your spiritual interests to the Savior who laid down His life for you, and of whom it is declared in Hebrews 7:25 that He is "able to save to the uttermost all who come unto God by Him?"

Surely, surely, dear believer, you, whose very name "believer" implies that you can believe, you will never again dare to excuse yourself on the plea of having no faith. For when you say this, you mean, of course, that you have no faith in God since you are not asked to have faith in yourself. Your soul would be in very poor condition indeed. Let me beg you, then, when you think or say these things, always to complete the sentence, and say, "I have no faith in—God! I can't believe—God!" I am sure this will soon become so dreadful to you, that you will not dare to continue it.

However, you say that you cannot believe without the Holy Spirit. Very well. Will you then come to the conclusion that your lack of faith is because of the failure of the Holy Spirit to do His work? For if it is, then you are surely not to blame and need feel no condemnation. All urgings for you to believe are useless.

But no! Don't you see that in saying you have no faith and cannot believe, you are not only "making God a liar," but you are also showing an utter lack of confidence in the Holy Spirit?

He is always ready to help our infirmities. We never have to wait for Him, He is always waiting for us. And I have such absolute confidence in the Holy Spirit and in His being always ready to do His work, that I dare to say to everyone of you, that you *can* believe now, at this very moment. If you do not, it is not the Spirit's fault, but your own.

Put your will, then, on the believing side. Say, "Lord, I will believe, I do believe," and continue to say it. Insist upon believing in the face of every doubt that assails you. Out of your unbelief, throw yourself completely on the Word, (the promises of God), and dare to abandon yourself to the keeping and saving power of the Lord Jesus. If you have ever trusted a friend for an important matter, I beg you, trust yourself and all your spiritual interests in the hands of your heavenly Friend now, and never allow yourself to doubt again.

Cease To Worry

Always remember that there are two things which are more completely incompatible than even oil and water. They are trust and worry. Would you call it trust to give something into the hands of a friend to take care of for you, and then spend your nights and days in anxious thought and worry as to whether it would be done correctly? And can you call it trust, when you have given the saving and keeping of your soul into the hands of the Lord, if day after day, and night after night, you are spending hours of anxious thought questioning the matter?

When a believer really trusts anything, he ceases to worry about the thing he has trusted. And when he worries, it is plain proof that he doesn't trust. Tested by this rule, how little real trust there is in the Church of Christ! No wonder our Lord asked the pathetic question in Luke 18:8, "When the Son of Man cometh, shall He find faith on the earth?" He will find plenty of work, a great deal of sincerity, and doubtless many consecrated hearts. But shall He find faith—the one thing He values more than all the rest? Every child of God will know how to answer this question regarding himself. If any of you still say "No," I beg you to let this be the last time for such an answer. If you have ever experienced the trustworthiness of our Lord, from now on believe that He is true, by the generous recklessness of your trust in Him!

Very early in my Christian life, I remember having every tender and loyal impulse within me stirred to the depths when I read an appeal in a volume of old sermons. The appeal called all who loved the Lord Jesus, to show others how worthy He was of being trusted by the steadfastness of their own faith in Him. As I read the inspiring words, I had a sudden glimpse of the privilege and the glory of being called to walk in paths so dark that only an utter recklessness of trust would be possible!

It may be true that "Ye have not passed this way heretofore" (Joshua 3:4). But today it is your happy privilege to prove your loyal confidence in Jesus, by starting out with Him on a life and walk of faith, lived moment by moment in absolute and child-like trust in Him.

You have trusted Him in a few things, and He has not failed you. Trust Him now for everything, and see if He does not do for you more than you could ever have asked or even thought. And remember that it is not done according to your power or capacity, but according to His own mighty power working in you all the good pleasure of His most blessed will.

You do not find it difficult to trust the management of the universe and all outward creations to the Lord. Can your own case be more complex and difficult than these, that you have to be anxious or troubled about His management of you? Get rid of such doubts! Take your stand on the power and trustworthiness of your God. See how quickly all difficulties will vanish before a steadfast determination to believe. Trust God always and you will find the faith that perhaps begins by a mighty effort, will end, sooner or later, by becoming the easy and natural habit of the soul. A law of the spiritual life is that every act of trust makes the next act less difficult. And at last, if you persist in these acts of trust, trusting becomes like breathing—the natural unconscious action of the redeemed soul.

Believe All God's Promises

Put your will into your believing. Your faith must not be passive. Your faith must be active energy. Be firmly resolved and say, "I will believe. I will not be discouraged." "For we are made partakers of Christ, if we hold the beginning of our

73

confidence (faith) steadfast unto the end" (Hebrews 3:14). They begin to build a little faith, but then begin to doubt. When we give in to doubts, we cannot have faith! We are told "all things are possible to him that believeth" (Mark 9:23). In Hebrews 11:33,34, we see that faith has subdued kingdoms, wrought righteousness, obtained promises, stopped the mouths of lions, quenched the violence of fire, escaped the edge of the sword, waxed valiant in fight, turned to flight the armies of the aliens. The Word assures us that faith can do it again. Our Lord Himself says, "If ye have faith as a grain of mustard seed, ye shall say unto this mountain, Remove hence to yonder place; and it shall remove; and nothing shall be impossible unto you" (Matthew 17:20).

If you are a child of God, you must have at least as much faith as a grain of mustard seed. Therefore, you dare not say again that you cannot trust because you have no faith. Instead, you should say, "I can trust my Lord, and I will trust Him. All the powers of earth or hell will not be able to make me doubt my wonderful, glorious, faithful Redeemer!"

Let your faith believe all of God's promises. In every dark hour remember: "Though now for a season, if need be, ye are in heaviness through manifold temptations" (1 Peter 1:6), be patient and trustful, and wait. First Peter 1:7 encourages us "that the trial of your faith, being much more precious than of gold that perisheth, though it be tried with fire, might be found unto praise and honour and glory at the appearing of Jesus Christ.''

Chapter 7

DIFFICULTIES CONCERNING THE WILL

When the child of God completely trusts the Lord for all areas of his life, and begins to know something of the blessedness of the life hid with Christ in God he may face a difficulty. If his experiences of peace and rest have somewhat subsided, or if he has never experienced them, he begins to feel that his situation is unreal. He begins to feel like a hypocrite. It seems to him that his belief does not go below the surface. It appears to be mere lip-belief. Therefore, he thinks it is of no account, and that his surrender is not a surrender of the heart and consequently cannot be acceptable to God. He is afraid to say he is completely the Lord's, for fear he will be telling an untruth. Yet he cannot bring himself to say he is not the Lord's because he longs for it so intensely. The difficulty is real and very disheartening.

This can be overcome when the Christian thoroughly understands the principles of the new life, and has learned *how* to live in it. The common thought is that this life hid with Christ in God is to be lived in the realm of emotions. Consequently, all the attention of the soul is directed toward the emotions. Whether the soul is at rest or troubled depends on whether the emotions are satisfied or not. Now, the higher Christian life is not to be lived in the emotions at all, but in the will. If the will of the Christian abides in the center of God's will the varying states of emotion do not disturb or affect the reality of the life in the least.

Fenelon makes this clear by stating: "pure religion resides in the will alone." He means that the will is the governing power in man's nature and, if the will is God-directed, all the rest of man's nature must come into harmony. When I speak of the will, I do not mean the wish of the man, or even his purpose, but the deliberate choice, the *deciding power* to which all that is in the man must yield obedience.

Choose To Believe

The emotions are sometimes thought to be the governing power in our nature. But I think all of us know as a matter of practical experience, that there is something within us, behind our emotions and our wishes, an independent self that decides everything and controls everything. Our emotions belong to us. We endure them and enjoy them, but they are not truly "us". If God is to take possession of us, He must enter into this central will or personality. As He reigns there by the power of His Spirit, all the rest of our nature must come under His sway. As the will is, so is the man.

This truth is very important. The decisions of our will are often directly opposed to the decisions of your emotions. If we are in the habit of considering our emotions as the test, we will feel like hypocrites in declaring those things to be real which our will alone has decided. But the moment we see that the will rules, we will completely disregard anything that goes against it. We will claim the decisions of the will as reality. Let the emotions rebel as they may.

I am aware that this is a difficult subject to deal with. But it is so practical regarding the life of faith that I beg you to master it.

Perhaps an illustration will help you. An intelligent young man seeking to enter into this new life was completely discouraged at finding himself the slave to the habit of doubting. Nothing seemed "true" or "real" to his emotions. The more he struggled, the more unreal it all became. He was told a secret concerning the will: if he would only choose to believe he need not then trouble about his emotions, for they would find themselves compelled, sooner or later, to come into harmony with the will. "What!" he said, "do you mean to tell me that I can *choose* to believe when nothing seems true to me? And will that kind of believing be real?" "Yes," was the answer. "It will. Fenelon says that true religion resides in the will alone. He means that, since a man's will is really the man's self, what his will does, he does. Your part is simply to put your will in this matter of believing over on God's side. Make up your mind that you will believe what He says, because He says it, and that you will not pay any attention to the feelings that make it seem so unreal. God will not fail to respond, sooner or later, to his revelation to such faith."

The young man paused a moment, and then solemnly said, "I understand, and will do what you say. I cannot control my emotions, but I can control my will. The new life begins to look possible to me if only my will needs to be set straight in the matter. I can give my will to God, and I do ."

From that moment, disregarding his emotions which continually accused him of being a hypocrite, this young man held firmly to the decision of his will. Instead of paying attention to his emotions, he continued to choose to believe. At the end of a few days, he found himself triumphant. Every emotion and every thought was brought into captivity to the power of the Spirit of God who had taken possession of the will put into His hands. The young man had firmly *professed* his faith without wavering. At times it took all the will power he possessed to say that he believed, because his senses and emotions did not support the fact. But he had understood the idea that his will was, after all, himself, and that if he kept his will on God's side, he was doing all he could do. God alone could change his emotions or control his being. The result has been one of the strongest Christian lives I know of, in its marvelous simplicity, directness, and power over sin.

A Surrendered Will

Here is the secret. Our will is the source of all our actions. Under the control of sin and self, our will caused us to act for our own pleasure. But God calls us to yield our wills to Him so He can take control of them and work in us to will and to do of His good pleasure. If we will obey this call and present ourselves to Him as a living sacrifice, He will take possession of our surrendered wills, and will begin at once to work in us, "that which is well pleasing in His sight, through Jesus Christ" (Hebrews 13:21), giving us the mind that was in Christ, and transforming us into His image (see Romans 12:1,2).

Here is another illustration. A lady who had entered into this life hid with Christ was facing a great trial. If she had listened to her emotions she would have been discouraged. But she had learned the secret of the will, and knowing that she had chosen the will of God for her portion, she didn't pay the slightest attention to her emotions. She persisted in confronting every thought concerning the trial with the words, "Thy will be done! Thy will be done!" That His will should be done was her delight! The result was that in an incredibly short space of time every thought was brought into captivity, and she began to find even her emotions rejoicing in the will of God.

There was another lady who had an habitual sin which her emotions dearly loved, but which in her will she hated. Believing herself to be under

80

the control of her emotions, she thought she was unable to conquer it, unless her emotions changed first. But she learned the secret concerning the will, and prayed, "Lord, you see that I love this sin emotionally, but in my real central self I hate it. Until now my emotions have had the mastery. But now I put my will into your hands, and give it up to your working. I will never again consent in my will to yield to this sin. Take possession of my will, and work in me to will and to do of your good pleasure."

Immediately she began to find deliverance. The Lord took possession of the will surrendered to Him and began to work in her by His own power. His will gained mastery over her emotions in the situation and she was delivered by the inward power of the Spirit of God.

Let me show you how to apply this principle to your own situation. Do not consider your emotions. They are only servants. Simply regard your will, which is the real ruler of your being. Is your will given up to God? Is your will put into His hands? Does your will decide to believe? Does your will choose to obey? If this is the case, then you are in the Lord's hands. You decide to believe, and you choose to obey. Your will is yourself. The thing is done. The transaction with God is real when your will acts. It is real in God's sight. Get hold of this secret. Discover that you do not need to pay attention to your emotions. You must simply pay attention to the state of your will.

"Yield yourself to God" (Romans 6:13). "Present yourself a living sacrifice to Him" (Romans 12:1). "Abide in Christ" (John 15:4). "Walk in the light" (1 John 1:7). All these Scripture commands become possible for you because you are aware that your will can act and can take God's side. Whereas, if you had to rely on your uncontrollable emotions, you would sink down in helpless despair.

When this feeling of unreality or hypocrisy comes, do not be troubled by it. It is only in your emotions and is not worth a moment's thought. Only see to it that your will is in God's hands. See that your inward self is abandoned to His working, that your choice, your decision, is on His side. Then leave it there. Your uncontrollable emotions, attached to the mighty power of God by the choice of your will must inevitably come into captivity and give their allegiance to Him.

Will What God Wills

The will is like a wise mother in a nursery. The emotions are like crying children. The mother makes up her mind to have her children do what she believes to be right and best. The children complain and say they won't do it. However, the mother knows that she is the one in control and pursues her course lovingly and calmly in spite of all their complaints. The result is that the children are sooner or later won over to the mother's course of action. They fall in with her decision and all is harmonious and happy. But if for a moment that mother should think that the children were the masters instead of herself, confusion would reign. At this very moment there are many who are confused, simply because their feelings are allowed to govern instead of their will.

Remember that the real thing in your experience is what your will decides, not what your emotions decide. You are in far more danger of hypocrisy and untruth in giving in to your feelings, than in holding firm to the decision of your will. If your will is on God's side, you are no hypocrite in claiming at this moment the blessed reality of belonging completely to Him, even though your emotions are not in agreement.

I am convinced that throughout the Bible the expressions concerning the "heart" do not mean the emotions (that which we now understand by the word "heart"). Rather, they mean the will, man's own central self. The object of God's dealing with man is that this "I" may be yielded up to Him, and this central life given up to His total control. It is not the feelings of the man God wants, but the man himself.

We must be careful not to make a mistake here. I say we must "give up" our wills, but I do not mean we are to be left will-less. We are not to give up our wills in order to be left like limp nerveless creatures without any will at all. We are simply to put the higher, divine, mature will of God in place of our foolish, misdirected wills of ignorance and immaturity. If we put the emphasis on the word "our," we will understand it better. The will we are to give up is our will, as it is misdirected and separated from God's will. We are not to "give up" our will when it is one with God's will. For when our will is in harmony with His will, it would be wrong for us to give it up.

The child is required to give up the misdirected will that belongs to it as a child, and we cannot let it say "I will" or "I will not." But when its will is in harmony with ours, we want it to stand up for those beliefs and, according to conscience say "I will" or "I will not" with all the force of which it is capable.

When God is "working in us to will," we must be firmly resolved to carry out this will. We must respond with an emphatic "I will" to every "Thou shalt" of His. For God can only carry out His own will with us as much as we consent to it.

Have *you* consented? Are you firmly resolved to will what God wills? He wills that you should be entirely surrendered to Him, and He wills that you should trust Him perfectly. Do you will the same?

Chapter 8

DIFFICULTIES CONCERNING GUIDANCE

Now you have begun the life of faith. You have
given yourself to the Lord to be completely His.
You are now entirely in His hands to be molded
according to His own divine purpose, into a vessel
unto His honor. Your most earnest desire is to
follow Him wherever He may lead you. You want
to be pliable in His hands. You are trusting Him to
"work in you to will and to do of His good pleasure" (Phillipians 2:13). But you find a great difficulty here. You have not yet learned to know His
voice, and you are in great doubt and perplexity as
to what really is His will for you.

Perhaps God seems to be calling you to certain
paths. Perhaps friends who seem to be more
mature in the Christian life have implied that you
might be in error. You hesitate to disagree with
them for fear of making them angry. In your heart
you believe the Lord is telling you to do a particular thing, yet you are timid about doing that thing
because friends do not approve. You find yourself
plunged into great doubt and uneasiness. The fully

surrendered soul has a way out of all these difficulties. I would repeat that the soul must be *fully* surrendered because if any part of the will is held back from God, it is almost impossible to find out the mind of God in reference to that point. Therefore, you must first be sure that your purpose is truly to obey the Lord in every area of your life. If this is your purpose, your soul only needs to know the will of God in order to consent to it. Then you surely cannot doubt His willingness to make His will known and to guide you in the right paths. The Bible clearly states many promises in reference to this. For instance, John 10:3,4 says, "He calleth His own sheep by name, and leadeth them out. And when He putteth forth His own sheep, He goeth before them, and the sheep follow Him: for they know his voice." John 14:26 says, "But the Comforter, which is the Holy Ghost, whom the Father will send in my name, He shall teach you all things, and bring all things to your remembrance, whatsoever I have said unto you." And James 1:5 tells us, "If any of you lack wisdom, let him ask of God, that giveth to all men liberally, and upbraideth not; and it shall be given him."

With such declarations, we must believe that divine guidance is promised to us. Our faith must therefore confidently look for and expect it. This is most important. In James 1:6,7, we are told, "let him ask in faith, nothing wavering. For he that wavereth is like a wave of the sea driven with the wind and tossed. For let not that man think that he shall receive anything of the Lord."

Study these scriptures and do not let the slightest doubt shake your firm faith that divine guidance has has been promised. If you seek it, you are sure to receive it.

God Knows All

Next, you must remember that our God has all knowledge and all wisdom. Therefore, it is very possible that He may guide you into paths where He knows great blessings are waiting for you. Men cannot see what God sees. God knows all. His ways are not as man's ways. His thoughts are not as man's thoughts. He alone knows the end of things from the beginning and can judge what the results of any course of action may be. Thus, you might go against the loving wishes of even your dearest friends. Remember, the key is *complete* surrender of the will to God. Certainly, there are those friends who are mature Christians whom God will use at times to guide us. However, we must rely on God's Word first and foremost. We must surrender ourselves completely to God. We must hold nothing back. He is our guide first and foremost. His Word leads us to a closer walk with Him.

Study Luke 14:26-33 and similar passages. Learn that in order to be a disciple and follower of your Lord, you may be called upon to inwardly forsake all that you have, even father or mother, or brother or sister, or husband or wife. You may even have to give up the way of life you once cherished. Unless this possibility is clearly recognized, you will likely get into difficulty. The child of God who enters upon this life of obedience is sooner or later led into paths which meet with the disapproval of those he loves best. And unless he is prepared for this, and can trust the Lord through it all, he will scarcely know what to do.

But, these points having all been settled, we now question how God's guidance comes to us, and how we will be able to know His voice. He reveals His will to us in four ways: through the Scriptures, through providential circumstances, through the convictions of our own higher judgment, and through the inward impressions of the Holy Spirit on our minds. It is safe to say that God speaks where these four are in harmony. I present this as a foundation principle. His voice will always be in harmony with itself, no matter how many different ways He may speak. There may be many voices, but there can be only one message. If God tells me in one voice to do something or not to do something, He cannot possibly tell me the opposite in another voice. If the voices contradict the speakers cannot be the same. My rule for distinguishing the voice of God would be to bring it to the test and see whether the four points beginning this chapter are in agreement.

Guidance From The Bible

Look first to the Bible. If you are in doubt about any subject, you must first consult the Bible and see whether there is any law there to direct you. Until you have found and obeyed God's will as it is revealed in His Word, you must not expect nor ask for a separate, direct, personal revelation. A great many mistakes are made in the matter of guidance overlooking this simple rule. Where the Father has given us a clearly written direction about something, He will not, of course, give us a special revelation about that thing. If we fail to search out and obey the Scripture rule and look instead for an inward voice, we will open ourselves to delusions, and will inevitably get into error. No man, for instance, could expect or need any direct personal revelation to tell him not to steal, because God has already plainly declared His will about stealing in the Bible, His Holy Word. However, I have frequently met with Christians who have gone off into fanaticism as the result.

It is true that the Bible does not always give a rule for every specific course of action, and in these cases we need and must expect guidance in other ways. But the Bible is more clear about details than most people think, and there are not many important things for which the Bible does not give clear direction.

The matter of dress is presented in 1 Peter 3:3,4, and in 1 Timothy 2:9. The matter of conversation is presented in Ephesians 4:29 and 5:4. The matter of vengeance and standing up for our rights is presented in Romans 12:19-21, Matthew 5:38-48, and 1 Peter 2:19-21. The matter of forgiving one another is presented in Ephesians 4:32 and Mark 11:25,26. The matter of conformity to the world is presented in Romans 12:2, 1 John 2:15-17, and James 4:4. The matter of anxieties of every kind is presented in Matthew 6:25-34 and Philippians 4:6-7.

I only give these examples to show how full and practical Bible guidance is. If you find yourself confused about something, first search and see what it has to say on the subject. Ask God to make clear to you what is His mind by the power of His Spirit and through the Scriptures. You must obey what is clearly taught in the Bible. No special guidance will ever be given about a point on which the Scriptures are clear, nor could any guidance ever contradict the Scriptures.

It is important to remember that the Bible is a book of principles. We must be careful not to isolate Bible verses which may, in fact, go against Bible principles. Remember in the fourth chapter of Luke, Satan used isolated Bible verses to tempt Christ, while Christ resisted Satan by stating Bible principles.

If you do not find any principles in the Bible that will settle your special point of difficulty, you must then seek guidance in the other ways mentioned. God will surely present Himself to you, either by convicting your judgment, by providential circumstances, or by a clear inward impression. In all true guidance these four voices will agree for God cannot say in one voice what He contradicts in another. Therefore, if you have an impression of duty, you must see whether it agrees with Scripture, whether it agrees with your own higher judgment, and also whether a door opens to enable you to perform the duty.

Impressions In Guidance

If anyone of these tests fails, it is not safe to proceed. You must wait in quiet trust until the Lord shows you that His voice is speaking. Anything which is out of this divine harmony must be rejected as not coming from God. We must never forget that "impressions" can come from other sources as well as from the Holy Spirit. The strong personalities of those around us are the source of many of our impressions. Impressions also come out of our physical conditions. And finally, impressions come from Satan who tries to stop us from seeking a more mature Christian life. Ephesians 2:6 tells us that we are seated in "heavenly places in Christ Jesus." Ephesians 6:12 tells us that "we wrestle not against flesh and blood, but against principalities, against powers, against the rulers of the darkness of this world, against spiritual wickedness in high places."

These spiritual enemies, whoever or whatever they may be, must communicate with us by means of our spiritual faculties. Their voices will be, as the voice of God is, an inward impression made upon our spirits. Consequently, just as the Holy Spirit may tell us by impressions what the will of God is concerning us, these spiritual enemies will also tell us by impressions what their will is concerning us. They disguise themselves as "angels of light" who have come to lead us closer to God.

Many sincere children of God have been deluded into paths of extreme fanaticism, while thinking they were closely following the Lord the whole time. God, who sees the sincerity of all hearts, can and does, pity and forgive. Remember, it is not enough to have a "leading." We must find out the *source* of that leading before we give ourselves up to follow it. Be careful not to be deceived!

So we must first test our "leadings" by seeing if they agree with what the Bible says. When we study and meditate on God's Word, His laws are written on our hearts. Thus our judgment and common sense will be based on Biblical concepts. We must also test our "leadings" by this judgment and common sense that is enlightened by the Holy Spirit. This is "conviction."

Our impressions must also be tested by providential circumstances. If a "leading" is of God, the way will always open for it. Our Lord assures us of this when He says in John 10:4, "And when He putteth forth His own sheep, *He goeth before them,* and the sheep *follow* Him; for they know His voice." Notice here the expressions "goeth before," and "follow." The Lord goes before us to open a way, and we are to follow in the way opened to us. It is never a sign of a divine leading when the Christian insists on opening his own way, riding roughly over all opposing things. If the Lord "goes before" us, He will open the door for us. We will not need to batter down doors for ourselves.

A Desire Of The Heart

That God *cares* enough about us to desire to regulate the details of our lives is the strongest proof of love He could give. He lets us know just how to live and walk to please Him. We never care about the little details of people's lives unless we love them.

God's law, therefore, is only another name for God's love. The more that law descends into the details of our lives, the more sure we are of the depth and reality of the love. We can never know the full joy and privilege of the life hid with Christ in God until we have learned the lesson of a daily and hourly guidance.

God's promise is that He will work in us to will as well as to do His good pleasure. This means, that He will take possession of our will and work it for us. His suggestions will come to us, not so much as commands from the outside, but as desires springing up within us. They will originate in our will. We will feel as though we *desired* to do something not as though we *must*. In Hebrews 8:10 God says, "I will put my laws into their mind, and write them in their hearts."

Therefore, the way in which the Holy Spirit usually works in a full obedient soul, in regard to this direct guidance, is to impress upon the mind a wish or desire to do or to not do certain things. Our affection and understanding embrace God's laws and we are drawn to obey, instead of being driven to it. Ask Him to make His will clear to you.

Promise Him that you will obey Him. Be firm in the belief that He is guiding you according to His word. When in doubt, wait for His clear direction. Look and listen for His voice continually.

Trust Him above all else. Trust Him to make you forget the "leading" if it is not His will. Faith is greatly needed here. He has promised to guide. You have asked Him to do it. Now you must believe that He does, and must take what comes as being His guidance. No earthly parent or master could guide his children or servants if they refuse to take his commands as really being the expression of his will. God cannot guide those souls who never trust Him enough to believe it.

Above all, do not be afraid of this blessed life, lived hour by hour and day by day under the guidance of your Lord! If He seeks to bring you out of the world and into a very close relationship with Him, do not shrink from it. It is your most blessed privilege. Rejoice in it. Embrace it eagerly. Surrender all to the Lord so it can be yours.

Chapter 9

DIFFICULTIES CONCERNING DOUBTS

Many Christians are slaves to the persistent habit of doubting. I do not mean doubts about the existence of God or the truths of the Bible. Rather, they doubt the forgiveness of their sins, their hopes of heaven, and their own inward experience. They are in bondage to their habit of doubting as an alcoholic is in bondage to his habit of drinking. Every step of their spiritual progress is fearfully taken waiting for doubts to assail them.

These doubts make their lives miserable, their usefulness is severely limited, and their communion with God is continually broken. The soul's entrance into a life of faith does, in many cases, take it altogether out of the region where these doubts live and flourish, However, Satan will still try to cause the feet to stumble and the heart to fail, even when he cannot completely succeed in turning the believer back into the ways of a life of sin.

The word "believer" means, of course, one who "believes" yet there are many believers who have to confess that they have doubts. Doubting is such a universal habit, that the only fitting and descriptive name that could be given to many of God's children would have to be Doubter instead of Believer. In fact, most Christians resign themselves to their doubts, as to a sort of inevitable sickness from which they suffer, but which they feel is a part of the necessary discipline of this earthly life. They moan about their doubts as a man might moan about his rheumatism. They make themselves out to be "interesting cases" which require the tenderest sympathy and the utmost consideration.

This is too often true of believers who are earnestly longing for the life and walk of faith, and who are making many steps toward it. They have gotten rid of doubting the forgiveness of their sins and their salvation, but they haven't gotten rid of doubting! They simply shifted the habit to a higher platform. Perhaps they say, "Yes, I believe my sins are forgiven and I am a child of God through faith in Jesus Christ. I don't doubt this any more. But——." This "but" includes many doubts concerning most of the promises our Father has made to His children. They fight with these promises. They refuse to believe them until they can have more reliable proof of their being true rather than believing what the Bible clearly states. Then they wonder why they are walking in such darkness. They look upon themselves as martyrs, and groan under the peculiar spiritual conflicts they are enduring.

Doubting Displeases God

Spiritual conflicts! It would be better if we called them spiritual rebellions! Our fight is to be a fight of faith. The moment we give in to doubts, our fight ceases, and our rebellion begins.

I must speak out about this!

Just as I would pray with an alcoholic for deliverance from bondage, I would encourage those who are given to doubting to be delivered from the bondage of those doubts. I would tell each about the perfect deliverance which the Lord Jesus Christ has in store for them, and I would plead with all the power at my command to avail themselves of it and be free. I would not listen to their excuses for one moment, but would tell them, "You ought to be free, you must be free!"

Would you be able to tolerate the doubts of your children? Suppose one would come to you and say, "I am such a doubter that I cannot believe I am your child, or that you really love me." Yet how often we hear a child of God express doubts. In the sight of God, I verily believe doubting is in some cases as displeasing as lying. It certainly is more dishonoring to Him. It denies His truthfulness and defames His character. John says that "he that believeth not God hath made Him a liar" (1 John 5:10). It seems to me that hardly anything could be worse than to fasten on God the character of being a liar! Have you ever thought of *this* as the result of your doubting?

I remember once seeing the anger and sorrow of

a mother's heart deeply stirred by a little doubting on the part of one of her children. She had left her two little girls with me while she did some errands. One of them played contentedly until her mother came back. The other one first wondered whether her mother would remember to come back for her. She then was afraid that her mother would indeed forget to come back for her because she had been naughty. She worked herself into quite a state. I will not easily forget the look on that mother's face, when the weeping little girl told what was the matter with her. Grief, wounded love, anger, and pity were struggling within the mother. She hardly knew whether she or the child was more at fault that such doubts could be possible.

Such doubts might be possible with an earthly mother, but never, never with God. Again and again I remember this incident which has deeply taught me and compelled me not to give in to doubts about my Heavenly Father's love and care and remembrance of me.

Doubting is a great trial. Consider when you have given in to negative thoughts against those who have, as you think, injured you. You brooded over their unkindnesses and it made you wretched. But, it was not easy to give up doing so.

Doubting is like this. In your Christian experience all has not gone well. Perhaps you have been assailed by temptations and have given in to them. You then conclude that God has forsaken you and does not love you, and is indifferent to your welfare. You are convinced that you are too wicked for Him to care for, or too difficult for Him to manage!

You do not mean to blame Him, or accuse Him of injustice, for you feel that His indifference and rejection of you are fully deserved because of your unworthiness. Under the guise of viewing your own shortcomings, you indulge in your dishonoring doubts. Although you think you are doubting yourself, you are really doubting the Lord. You are indulging in wrong thoughts of Him. He declares that He came to save, not the righteous, but sinners. Instead of being a reason why He should not love you and care for you, your sinfulness and unworthiness are really your chiefest claim upon His love and His care. Jesus says, "They that are whole need not a physician, but they that are sick" (Luke 5:31). He also says in Luke 5:4, "What man of you, having an hundred sheep, if he lose one of them, doth not leave the ninety and nine in the wilderness, and go after that which is lost, until he find it?" Any thoughts that are different from what He Himself has said are wrong. They dishonor Him. It is always sinful to indulge in doubts throughout your Christian life. Doubts and discouragements come from Satan and are always untrue. A direct and emphatic denial is the only way to meet them.

Deliverance From Doubt

This brings me to the practical part of the whole subject—deliverance from this fatal habit. Deliv-

erance from this must be by the same means a
deliverance from any other sin. It is to be found in
Christ and in Him only. You must hand your
doubting over to Him as you have learned to hand
your other temptations. You must do with doubt
ing just what you do with your temper or your
pride. You must give it up to the Lord. Pledge not
to doubt as you would encourage an alcoholic to
pledge not to drink, trusting in the Lord alone to
keep you steadfast.

Like any other sin, the stronghold is in the will
and the will or purpose to doubt must be surren
dered exactly as you surrender the will or purpose
to yield to any other temptation. God always takes
possession of a surrendered will. If we come to
the point of saying that we will not doubt, and
surrender our wills to Him, His blessed Spirit will
begin at once to "worketh in (us) both to will and
to do of His good pleasure" (Philippians 2:13)
and we will find ourselves kept from doubting by
His mighty and overcoming power.

In this matter of doubting the trouble is that the
Christian does not always make a full surrender. "I
do not want to doubt any more," we will say, or
"I hope I will not." But it is hard to come to the
point of saying, "I *will* not doubt again," and no
surrender is effective until one says, "I will not."
We must give up doubting forever and must con
sent to a continuous life of trust.

Remember: we cannot give up doubting gradu
ally. We must give it up all at once and must com
pletely rely on the Lord for deliverance when we

are tempted. The moment the assault comes, we must lift up the shield of faith against it. We must hand the very first suggestion of doubt over to the Lord, and must let Him manage it. We must refuse to entertain the doubt a single moment. We must simply say, "I dare not doubt. I must trust. God *is* my Father, and He does love me. Jesus saves me. He saves me now." Those three little words, repeated over and over, "Jesus saves me, Jesus saves me," will put to flight the greatest army of doubts that ever assaulted any soul. I have tried it many times and have never known it to fail.

Pay no attention to your doubts. Treat them with the utmost contempt.Tell Jesus that you trust Him and that you intend to go on trusting Him. Hold fast to Him. You will then be able to join in the song of Moses and the children of Israel, saying, "I will sing unto the Lord, for He hath triumphed gloriously: the horse and his rider hath He thrown into the sea. The Lord is my strength and song, and He is become my salvation" (Exodus 15:1,2). When Satan tries to attack remember Isaiah 59:19 "the Spirit of the Lord shall lift up a standard against him," and your doubts will be put to flight.

Therefore, be determined to never doubt again. Make it a real transaction between your soul and the Lord. Tell Him all about your weakness and your long-encouraged habits of doubt. Tell Him how helpless you are before it. Commit the whole battle to Him. As it says in Hebrews 12:2, keep your face steadfastly "looking unto Jesus." Look away from yourself and away from your doubts.

Encourage yourself with Hebrews 10:23: "Let us hold fast the profession of our faith without wavering; (for He is faithful that promised)."

Rely on *His* faithfulness, not on your own. You have committed the keeping of your soul to Him and you must never again admit the possibility of His being unfaithful. Believe He is faithful, not because you feel it, or see it, but because He says He is. Cultivate a continuous habit of believing, and all doubt will vanish in the blaze of the glory of the absolute faithfulness of God.

"Thanks be to God, which giveth us the victory through our Lord Jesus Christ" (1 Corinthians 15:57.)

Chapter 10

DIFFICULTIES CONCERNING TEMPTATIONS

In the life of faith, some very great mistakes are made concerning the matter of temptation.

First of all, people seem to think that temptations will cease after one is saved. They think that they will be delivered from yielding to temptation and from being tempted. When temptations come they are completely discouraged. They think they must have gone wrong in some way.

They make the mistake of looking upon temptation as sin. Even though they hate the sin, they blame themselves for the suggestion brought about by the temptation. This brings them into condemnation and discouragement. A discouraged soul is an easy prey of sin, so that we often fall from the very fear of having fallen.

To meet the first of these difficulties, it is necessary to refer to the scriptures which state that the Christian life is to be one of warfare. It is especially so when we "sit together in heavenly places in Christ Jesus" (Ephesians 2:6). We are called to wrestle against spiritual enemies, whose power and skill to tempt us is far superior to any we have encountered before. "For we wrestle not against flesh and blood, but against principalities, against powers, against the rulers of the darkness of this world, against spiritual wickedness in high places" (Ephesians 6:12). In fact, temptations generally increase in strength after we have entered the higher Christian life. However, we must never suppose we have not really found the true abiding place. Strong temptations are often a sign of great grace.

When the children of Israel had first left Egypt, the Lord did not lead them through the country of the Philistines, although that was the nearest way. Exodus 13:17 tells us "for God said, Lest peradventure the people repent when they see war, and they return to Egypt." But afterwards, when they had learned how to trust Him better, He permitted their enemies to attack them. Even in their journey through the wilderness they met with few enemies, and fought few battles. But in the land of Canaan they had to conquer seven great nations and thirty-one kings, take walled cities, and overcome giants.

They could not have fought with the "Canaanites, and the Hittites, and the Amorites, and the Perizzites, and the Hivites, and the Jebusites" (Exodus 3:8), until they had gone into the land where these enemies were. The power of your temptations may be one of the strongest proofs that you really are in the land of promise. Consequently, you must never allow them to cause you to question that fact.

Temptation Is Not Sin

It is harder to deal with the second mistake often made regarding temptation. It hardly seems to be worth saying that temptation is not sin. Yet, much distress arises from not understanding this fact. Even the suggestion of doing wrong makes the poor tempted soul begin to feel as if it must be very bad indeed. The person feels that he or she must be far away from God to have had such thoughts and suggestions. It is as if a burglar should break into a man's house to steal, and when the master of the house begins to resist him and drive him out, the burglar turns around and accuses the owner of being the thief. This is Satan's great trick for entrapping us. He comes and whispers suggestions of evil to us—doubts, blasphemies, jealousies, envyings, and pride—and then turns around and says, "You are wicked to think such things! It is very plain that you are not trusting the Lord. For if you had been, it would be impossible for these things to have entered your heart." This reasoning sounds so plausible that we often accept it as true, come under condemnation, and are filled with discouragement. Then it is easy for temptation to develop into actual sin.

One of the most fatal things in the life of faith is discouragement. One of the most helpful is confidence. Someone once said that in overcoming temptations confidence was the first thing, confidence the second, and confidence the third. We must *expect* to conquer. That is why the Lord so often said to Joshua, "Be strong and of a good courage; be not afraid, neither be thou dismayed" (Joshua 1:9). "Only be thou strong and very courageous" (Joshua 1:7). It is also the reason He says to us, "Let not your heart be troubled, neither let it be afraid" (John 14:27). The power of temptation is to make our hearts faint. Satan knows this well and always begins his assaults by discouraging us in any way he can.

This discouragement sometimes arises from what we think is a righteous grief and disgust at ourselves that such things *could* be any temptation to us. However, we are really ashamed at the realization that we placed ourselves "above" being tempted. We are discouraged because we expected something from ourselves, and are sorely disappointed not to find something there. This shame and discouragement may appear to be true humility. However, they are really a far worse condition than the temptation itself, for they are nothing but the results of wounded self-love. True humility can bear to see its own weakness and foolishness revealed, because it never expected anything from itself and knows that its only hope and expectation must be in God. Therefore, instead of discouraging the humble soul from trusting, such revelations drive it to a deeper and more complete trust. But the counterfeit humility that self-love produces plunges the soul into the depths of a faithless discouragement and drives it into the very sin which distressed it.

The Source Of Temptation

There is a symbolic story that illustrates this wonderfully. Satan called together a council of his servants to consult how they might make a good man sin. One demon said, "I will make him sin." "How will you do it?" asked Satan. "I will set before him the pleasures of sin," was the reply. "I will tell him of its delights, and the rich rewards it brings." "Ah," said Satan, "that will not do. He has tried it and knows better than that." Another demon said, "I will make him sin." "What will you do?" asked Satan. "I will tell him of the pains and sorrows of virtue. I will show him that virtue has no delights, and brings no rewards." "Ah, no!" exclaimed Satan, "that will not do at all. He has tried it and knows that '(Wisdom's) ways *are* ways of pleasantness, and all her paths are peace' " (Proverbs 3:17). "Well," said another demon, "I will undertake to make him sin." "And what will you do?" asked Satan again. "I will discourage his soul," was the short reply. "Ah, that will do!" cried Satan. "That will do! We will conquer him now."

An old writer says, "All discouragement is from the devil." I wish every Christian would take this as a motto, and would realize that he must fight discouragement as he would sin.

But this is impossible if we fail to recognize the truth about temptation. If temptations were our own fault, we could not help being discouraged. But they are not. The Bible says, "Blessed is the man that endureth temptation" (James 1:12). We are strongly urged to "count it all joy when we fall into divers temptations" (James 1:2). Temptation, therefore, cannot be sin. The truth is, it is no more a sin to hear these whispers and suggestions of evil in our souls, than it is for us to hear the wicked talk of men as we pass along the street. In either case, the sin comes, only by our stopping and joining in with them. If we turn from wicked suggestions at once as we would turn from wicked talk, and pay no more attention to them than we would to the talk, we do not sin. But we sin if we dwell on them. We may be enticed by temptations a thousand times a day and not sin. We cannot help these enticings and are not to blame for them. But if we begin to think that these enticings are actual sin on our part, then the battle is already half lost, and the sin can easily gain a complete victory.

A dear lady in distress from not understanding this once came to me. She had been living very happily in the life of faith for some time, and had been so free from temptation that she began to think she would never be tempted again. But suddenly, a very peculiar form of temptation had assailed her which had horrified her. She found that the moment she began to pray, dreadful thoughts of all kinds would rush into her mind. She had lived a very sheltered, innocent life. These thoughts seemed so awful to her that she felt she must be one of the most wicked of sinners to be capable of having them. She began by thinking that she could not possibly have entered into the rest of faith, and ended by concluding that she had never even been born again. Her soul was in agony. I told her that these dreadful thoughts were purely and simply temptations, and that she herself was not to blame for them at all. She could not help them anymore than she could help hearing a wicked man pour out his blasphemies in her presence. I urged her to recognize and treat them only as temptations and not to blame herself or be discouraged, but rather to turn at once to the Lord and commit them to Him. I showed her how great an advantage Satan gained by making her think these thoughts originated with her, plunging her into condemnation and discouragement. I assured her she would find a speedy victory if she would pay no attention to them, ignore their presence, and simply turn her back on them and look to the Lord.

She grasped the truth, and the next time these blasphemous thoughts came, she rebuked Satan. She concentrated on the Lord, and Satan fled in confusion, and her soul was perfectly delivered.

Satan knows if he is recognized as the source of the temptation, the Christian will recoil from it far more quickly than if it seems to be the suggestion of his own mind. If the devil prefaced each temptation with the words "I am the devil, your relentless enemy. I have come to make you sin," I suppose we would hardly feel any desire at all to yield to his suggestions. He has to hide himself in order to make his baits attractive. Our victory will be more easily gained if we are not ignorant of his devices and recognize them at his very first approach.

More Than Conquerors

We also make another great mistake about temptations. We think that all time spent in combating them is lost. Hours pass and we seem to have made no progress because we have been so beset with temptations. But it often happens that we have been serving God far more truly during these hours than in our times of comparative freedom from temptation. For we are fighting our Lord's battles when we are fighting temptation, and hours are often worth days to us under these circumstances. We read, "Blessed is the man that *endureth* temptation" (James 1:12). I am sure this means enduring temptation that continues and recurs. Patience is cultivated when one endures temptation. Nothing so drives us to completely depend upon the Lord Jesus as the continuance of temptation. Nothing brings more praise and honor and glory to the Lord than the trial of our faith that comes through temptations. 1 Peter 1:7 tells us that it is "more precious than of gold. . .though it be tried with fire." James 1:12 says that we who patiently endure the trial, shall receive for our reward "the crown of life, which the Lord hath promised to them that love Him."

The Holy Spirit strongly urges us in James 1:2-4: "Count it all joy when ye fall into divers temptation; knowing this that the trying of your faith worketh, patience. But let patience have her perfect work, that ye may be perfect and entire, wanting nothing.''

Temptation is plainly one of the instruments used by God to complete our perfection. Thus, sin's own weapons are turned against itself, and we see how it is that all things (even temptations) can work together for good to them that love God.

Remember, the way to victory over temptation is faith. This is the foundation of the higher Christian life. Our one great motto should be: ''We are nothing. Christ is all.'' Always and everywhere start to stand, and walk, and overcome, and live by faith. We are utterly helpless and know that we cannot do anything for ourselves. We have learned that we must hand the temptation over to our Lord and trust Him to conquer it for us. But when we put it into His hands, we must *leave* it there. This is the greatest difficulty of all. It seems impossible to believe that the Lord can or will manage our temptations without our help, especially if they do not immediately disappear. To go on patiently ''enduring'' when a temptation continues, without yielding to it, and also without snatching ourselves out of the Lord's hand in regard to it, is a wonderful victory for our impatient natures. But it is a victory we must gain if we would do what will please God.

We must commit ourselves to the Lord for victory over our temptations as we committed ourselves at first for forgiveness. We must leave ourselves completely in His hands for both.

Thousands of God's children have done this and

can today testify that marvelous victories have been gained over temptations. They have in very truth been made "more than conquerors" through Him who loves them.

Chapter 11

DIFFICULTIES CONCERNING FAILURES

The title of this chapter may startle some readers. "Failures," they will say. "We thought there were no failures in this life of faith!"

I would answer that there should not be failures and need not be failures, but there sometimes are failures, and we must deal with facts and not with theories. Teachers of this interior life do not say that it becomes impossible to sin. They only insist that sin ceases to be a necessity, and a possibility of continual victory is opened before us. There are very few, if any, who do not confess to have at times been overcome by at least a momentary temptation.

I am speaking of conscious, known sin. I am not talking about the subject of sins of ignorance, or what is called the inevitable sin of our nature. These are all met by the provisions of Christ, and do not disturb our fellowship with God. I have no desire nor ability to discuss the doctrines concerning sin. I will leave the theologians to discuss and settle these. I speak only of the believer's experience in the matter.

There are many things which we do innocently enough until an increasing light shows them to be wrong. These may all be classed under sins of ignorance. Since they are done in ignorance they do not bring us under condemnation and do not come within the range of the present discussion.

An example of this once occurred in my presence. A little baby girl was playing one warm summer afternoon, while her father was resting on the lounge. A bottle of ink on the table got the child's attention, and unnoticed by anyone, she climbed on a chair and took it. Then, walking over to her father with an air of childish triumph, she turned it upside down on his white shirt and laughed with glee as she saw the black streams trickling down on every side.

This was very wrong for the child to do, but it could not be called sin because she knew no better. Had she been older, and understood that bottles of ink were not playthings, it would have been wrong. "To him that knoweth to do good, and doeth it not, to him it is sin" (James 4:17). In all I say concerning sin in this chapter, I desire it to be fully understood that I refer simply to that which comes within the range of our consciousness.

Identifying Sin

Misunderstanding on the point of known or conscious sin opens the way for great dangers in the life of faith. When a believer trusts that he has entered upon the highway of holiness and then finds himself surprised into sin, he is tempted to be either completely discouraged and to give everything up as lost, or, to cover up his sins and refuse to be honest about it. Either of these courses is equally fatal to any real growth and progress in the life of holiness. The only way is to face the fact at once, identify it as sin, and discover, if possible, the reason and the remedy. This life of union with God requires complete honesty with Him and with ourselves. The blessing that the sin would only momentarily disturb is sure to be lost by any dishonest dealing with it. A sudden failure is no reason for being discouraged and giving up all as lost. Neither is the integrity of the higher Christian life affected by it. We are not preaching a *state,* but a *walk.* The highway of holiness is not a *place,* but a *way.* Sanctification is not a thing to be picked up at a certain stage of our experience, and possessed forever after, but it is a life to be lived day by day and hour by hour. We may turn aside from a path for a moment, but the path is not obliterated by our leaving it and can be instantly regained. In this life and walk of faith, there may be momentary failures that need not disturb the attitude of the soul regarding entire consecration, perfect trust, its happy communion with its Lord.

To instantly turn back to God is the great point here. Our sin is no reason for stopping to trust. It only proves that we must trust more fully than ever. Discouragement offers no remedy no matter what the cause of sin. As a child who is learning to walk might lie down in despair when he has fallen and refuse to take another step, so this believer, who is seeking to learn how to live and walk by faith, gives up in despair because of having fallen into sin. In either case, get right up and try again. When the children of Israel had met with disastrous defeat before the little city of Ai soon after their entrance into the land, they were so completely discouraged that we read in Joshua 7:5-9: "Wherefore the hearts of the people melted, and became as water. And Joshua rent his clothes, and fell to the earth upon his face before the ark of the Lord until the eventide, he and the elders of Israel, and put dust upon their heads. And Joshua said, Alas, O Lord God, wherefore hast Thou at all brought this people over Jordan, to deliver us into the hand of the Amorites, to destroy us? Would to God we had been content, and dwelt on the other side Jordan! O Lord, what shall I say, when Israel turneth their backs before their enemies! For the Canaanites and all the inhabitants of the land shall hear of it and shall environ us round, and cut off our name from the earth: and what will Thou do unto Thy great name?"

What a wail of despair this was! And how exactly it is repeated by many a child of God today, whose heart, because of a defeat, melts and becomes as water. He or she is set for further failures and shows a lack of trust in God like the Israelites. No doubt Joshua thought then, as we are likely to think now, that discouragement and despair naturally result after such a failure. But God thought otherwise. In Joshua 7:10 we read: "And the Lord said unto Joshua, Get thee up, wherefore liest thou thus upon thy face?" The proper thing to do, was not to abandon themselves to discouragement, humble as it might look, but to face the evil at once and get rid of it, and immediately to sanctify themselves.

Confess Sin Immediately

"Up, sanctify the people" (Joshua 7:13) is always God's command. "Lie down and be discouraged," is always our temptation. Our feeling is that it is presumptuous, and almost impertinent, to go at once to the Lord after having sinned against Him. It seems as if we first ought to suffer the consequences of our sin for a little while and endure the accusation of our conscience. We can hardly believe that the Lord *can* be willing at once to receive us back into loving fellowship with Him.

A little girl once expressed this feeling to me, with a child's honesty. She asked whether the Lord Jesus always forgave us for our sins as soon as we asked Him, and I said, "Yes, of course He does." *"Just* as soon?" she repeated doubtingly. "Yes," I replied, "the very minute we ask, He forgives us." "Well," she said deliberately, "I can't believe that. I should think He would make us feel sorry for two or three days first. And then I should think He would make us ask Him a great many times, and in a very pretty way too, not just in common talk. And I believe that *is* the way He does, and you need not try to make me think He forgives me right at once, no matter what the Bible says."

She only *said* what most Christians *think,* and what is worse, what most Christians act on, making their discouragement and their remorse separate them further from God than their sin would have done. Yet it is so totally contrary to the way we like our own children to act toward us, that I wonder how we ever could have conceived such an idea about God. How a mother grieves when a naughty child goes off alone in remorse, and doubts her willingness to forgive. How her whole heart goes out in welcoming love to the repentant little one who runs to her at once and begs her forgiveness! Surely our God felt this yearning love when He said to us, "Return, ye backsliding children, and I will heal your backsliding" (Jeremiah 3:22).

The same moment that we become aware of sin, we also ought to confess our sin and receive forgiveness. This is especially important to an unwavering walk in the "life hid with Christ in God," for no separation from Him can be tolerated here for an instant.

We can only walk this path by "Looking (continually) unto Jesus" (Hebrews 12:2), moment by moment. If our eyes turn away from Him to look upon our own sin and our weakness, we will leave the path at once. The believer who seeks the higher Christian life and finds himself overcome by sin, must flee with it instantly to the Lord. He must act on 1 John 1:9, "If we confess our sins, He is faithful and just to forgive us our sins, and to cleanse us from all unrighteousness." The believer must not hide his sin and seek to excuse it. Nor should he let time push it out of his memory. He must confess his sin and put it away from him. He must believe, then and there, that God *is* faithful and just to forgive him his sin, that He does do it, and further, that He also cleanses him from all unrighteousness. He must by faith claim an immediate forgiveness and an immediate cleansing, and must go on trusting harder and more absolutely than ever.

As soon as Israel's sin had been brought to light and put away, at once God's word came again in a message of glorious encouragement: "Fear not, neither be thou dismayed. . . .See, I have given into. thy hand the king of Ai, and his people, and his city, and his land" (Joshua 8:1). Our courage must rise higher than ever. We must abandon ourselves more completely to the Lord, that His mighty power may more perfectly work in us. Moreover, we must forget our sin as soon as it is confessed and forgiven. We must not dwell on it, and examine it, and indulge in distress and remorse. We must not put it on a pedestal and then walk around it and view it on every side, magnifying it into a mountain that hides God from our eyes. We must follow Paul's example and, "forgetting those things which are behind, and reaching forth unto those things which are before," we must "press toward the mark for the prize of the high calling of God in Christ Jesus"

(Philippians 3:13,14).

Examples Of Temptation

Let me give two contrasting examples. The first concerns a sincere Christian man who was an active worker in the Church, and who had been living for several months in an experience of great peace and joy. He was suddenly overcome by a temptation to treat a brother unkindly. Having supposed it to be an impossibility that he could ever sin that way again, he was plunged at once into the deepest discouragement, and concluded he had been altogether mistaken and had never entered into the life of full trust at all. Day by day his discouragement increased until it became despair. He concluded that he had never even been born again and gave himself up for lost. He spent three years of utter misery, going farther and farther away from God, being gradually drawn off into one sin after another, until his life was a curse to himself and to all those around him. His health failed under the terrible burden, and there were fears for his sanity.

At the end of three years, he met a Christian lady who understood this truth about sin that I have been trying to explain. After speaking with him a few moments, she found out his trouble, and said at once, "You sinned, there is no doubt about it, and I don't want you to try to excuse it. But have you never confessed it to the Lord and asked Him to forgive you?" "Confessed it!" he exclaimed, "why, it seems to me I have done nothing but confess it and beg God to forgive me, night and day these three dreadful years." "And you have never believed He did forgive you?" asked the lady. "No," said the poor man, "how could I, for I never *felt* as if He did?" "But suppose He had said He forgave you, wouldn't that have done as well for you to feel it?" "Oh yes," replied the man; "if God said it, of course I would believe it." "Very well, He does say so," was the lady's answer. She turned to the verse mentioned earlier (1 John 1:9) and read it aloud. "Now," she continued, "you have been confessing and confessing your sin for three years, and all the while God says in the Bible that He was faithful and just to forgive it and to cleanse you. Yet you never once believed it. Remember 1 John 5:10 says: "he that believeth not God hath made Him a liar.""

The poor man saw the whole thing and was amazed. When the lady suggested that they should kneel down, he obeyed and confessed his past unbelief and sin. He claimed, then and there, a present forgiveness and a present cleansing. The result was glorious. The darkness of his soul gave way to light and he began to praise God aloud for the wonderful deliverance. In a few minutes his soul was once more resting in the Lord and rejoicing in the fullness of His salvation.

The other example concerns the case of a Christian lady seeking the higher Christian life, who had a very bright and victorious experience. Some time later, she was suddenly overcome by a violent burst of anger. A flood of discouragement swept over her soul for a moment. The temptation came as this, "There now, that shows it was all a mistake. Of course you have been deceived about the whole thing and have never entered into the life of faith at all. And now you may as well give up altogether, for you never can entirely consecrate yourself more fully nor trust more fully than you did this time. It is very plain, this life of holiness is not for you!" These thoughts flashed through her mind in a moment. But she was taught well in the ways of God, and she said at once, "Yes, I have sinned, and it is very sad. But the Bible says that if we confess our sins God is faithful and just to forgive us our sins, and to cleanse us from all unrighteousness. And I believe He will do it." She did not delay a moment, but while still boiling over with anger, she ran into a room where she could be alone. Kneeling down beside the bed she said, "Lord, I confess my sin. I have sinned. I hate it, but I can't get rid of it. I confess it to You with shame and confusion. And now I believe according to Your Word, that You do forgive me and cleanse me from this." She said it out loud, for the inward turmoil was too great for it to be said inside. As the words "You do forgive me and cleanse me from this" passed her lips, the deliverance came. The Lord said, "Peace, be still!" and there was a great calm. A flood of light and joy burst on her soul. The enemy fled, and she was more than conquered through Him that loved her. Her sin, confession, and recovery did not even take five minutes, and her feet were planted more firmly than ever on the blessed highway of holiness. She sang her song of deliverance with deeper meaning "I will sing unto the Lord, for He hath triumphed gloriously" (Exodus 15:1).

In every emergency the only remedy is to trust in the Lord. And if this is all we ought to do, and all we can do, isn't it better to do it at once? And I have realized the folly of seeking deliverance in any other way, by saying to myself, "I will have to trust in the end. Why not trust at once, in the beginning." We have entered upon a life and walk of faith. If we fail in this life and walk of faith, our only recovery must lie in an increase of faith, not in a lessening of it.

Let every failure drive you instantly to the Lord with a more complete abandonment and a more perfect trust. And if you do this, you will find that although it is sad to have failed, the failure has not broken your sweet communion with Him for long.

Where failure is met in this way, a recurrence is far more likely to be prevented than where the soul allows itself to pass through a season of despair and remorse. If failure should sometimes recur, and is always treated in the same way, it is sure to become less and less frequent, until it finally stops altogether. There are some happy souls who learn the whole lesson at once. But the blessing is also upon those who take slower steps and gain a more gradual victory.

Causes Of Failure

Having discussed the way to be delivered from

123

failure, I would now like to say a bit about the causes of failure in this deeper walk. The causes do not lie in the strength of the temptation nor do they lie in our own weakness, or in any lack in the power or willingness of our Savior to save us. The promise to Israel was positive: "There shall not any man be able to stand before thee all the days of thy life" (Joshua 1:5). The promise to us is equally positive: "God is faithful, who will not suffer you to be tempted above that ye are able; but will with the temptation also make a way to escape, that ye may be able to bear it" (1 Corinthians 10:13).

In the book of Joshua, we read that the people who had conquered the mighty Jericho "fled before the men of Ai" (Joshua 7:4). They didn't flee because of the strength of their enemy, nor did they flee because God failed them. The cause of their defeat lay somewhere else, and the Lord Himself declares it: "Israel hath sinned, and they have also transgressed My covenant which I commanded them: for they have even taken of the accursed thing, and have also stolen, and dissembled also, and they have put it even among their own stuff. Therefore the children of Israel could not stand before their enemies, but turned their backs before their enemies" (Joshua 7:11,12). It was a hidden evil that conquered them. Buried under the earth in an obscure tent in that vast army was hidden something against which God had a controversy. And this little hidden thing made the whole army helpless before their enemies. In

Joshua 7:13 we read, "There is an accursed thing in the midst of thee, O Israel: thou canst not stand before thine enemies, until ye take away the accursed thing from among you."

The lesson here is simply this, that anything cherished in the heart which is contrary to the will of God, be it ever so insignificant or deeply hidden, will cause us to fall before our enemies. Any conscious root of bitterness cherished toward another, any self-seeking, any harsh judgments, any slackness in obeying the voice of the Lord, any doubtful habits or surroundings will effectually cripple and paralyze our spiritual life. We may have hidden the evil in the most remote corner of our heart. We may have even hidden from our own sight and refused to even recognize its existence, although we cannot help being secretly aware that it is there all the time. We may steadily ignore it, and persist in declarations of consecration and full trust. We may be more earnest than ever in our religious duties. We may have the eyes of our understanding opened more and more to the truth and the beauty of the life and walk of faith. We may seem to ourselves and to others to have reached a solid position of victory. Yet, we may find ourselves suffering bitter defeats. We may wonder, question, despair, and pray. Nothing will do any good until the sin is dug up from its hiding place, brought out to the light, and laid before God.

When a believer who is walking in this interior life meets with a defeat, he must look for the cause at once. He is not to look at the strength of the enemy, but in something behind—some hidden lack of consecration lying at the very center of his being. Just as a headache is not itself the disease but only a symptom of a disease situated in some other part of the body, so the failure in such a Christian is only the symptom of an evil, hidden in probably a very different part of his nature.

Sometimes the evil may be hidden in what looks like good. A judging spirit or a subtle leaning to our own understanding may be hidden beneath apparent zeal for the truth. An absence of Christian love may be hidden beneath apparent Christian faithfulness. A great lack of trust in God may be hidden beneath an apparently rightful care for our affairs. I believe our blessed Guide, the indwelling Holy Spirit, is always secretly revealing these things to us by continual pangs of conscience, (convictions), so that we are left without excuse for hiding the sin. But it is very easy to disregard His gentle voice and tell ourselves that all is right, while the fatal evil continues to be hidden in our midst, causing defeat in the most unexpected quarters.

Secret Corners Of Sin

Here is a good example of this. We moved into a new house, and in looking it over to see if it was all ready for occupancy, I noticed in the cellar a very clean looking cider barrel headed up at both ends. I thought that perhaps I should take it out of the cellar and see what was in it, but I decided to leave it undisturbed. It seemed to be empty and looked clean, and it would have been quite a piece of work to get it up the stairs. I didn't feel at peace about it, but left it anyway. When house cleaning time came every spring and fall, I would remember that barrel with a little twinge of housewifely conscience, feeling I could not quite rest in the thought of a perfectly clean house while the barrel remained unopened, perhaps containing some hidden evil. Still, I managed to quiet my conscience, thinking of the trouble it would take to investigate it.

For two or three years the innocent looking barrel stood quietly in our cellar. Then, without apparent reason, moths began to fill our house. In vain I tried to get rid of them. They increased rapidly and threatened to ruin everything we had. I suspected the carpets were the cause, and subjected them to a thorough cleaning. I suspected our furniture, too, and had it newly upholstered. I suspected all sorts of impossible things. At last the thought of the barrel came to me. At once I had it brought out of the cellar. When the head was knocked in, I think it safe to say that thousands of moths poured out. The previous occupant of the house must have had something in it which breeds moths, and this was the cause of all my trouble.

In the same way I believe that some innocent looking habit or indulgence, some apparently unimportant thing, lies at the root of most of the failure in this interior life. *All* is not given up. Some secret corner is kept locked against the Lord.

Some evil thing is hidden in the recesses of our hearts, and so we cannot stand before our enemies.

In order to prevent failure, or to discover its cause if we have failed, it is necessary to keep continually before us this prayer: "Search me, O God, and know my heart: try me, and know my thoughts: And see if there be any wicked way in me, and lead me in the way everlasting" (Psalm 139:23,24).

Do not think that I believe in failure because I have said all this about it. There is no necessity for it at all. The Lord Jesus *is* able to deliver us out of the hands of our enemies that we may "serve Him without fear. In holiness and righteousness before Him, all the days of our life" (Luke 1:74,75). Let us then pray, every one of us, day and night, "Lord, keep us from sinning and make us living witnesses of Your mighty power to save us to the uttermost." Let us never be satisfied until we are pliable in His hands and have learned to trust Him. We are told in Hebrews 13:21, He will be able to "Make (us) perfect in every good work to do His will, working in (us) that which is well pleasing in His sight, through Jesus Christ; to whom be glory for ever and ever. Amen!"

Chapter 12

IS GOD IN EVERYTHING?

One of the greatest obstacles to an unwavering experience in the interior life is the difficulty of seeing God in everything. People say, "I can easily submit to things that come from God. But I cannot submit to man which is the source of most of my trials." Or they say, "It is all well enough to talk of trusting. But when I commit a matter to God, man is sure to come in and cause problems. While I have no difficulty in trusting God, I do see serious difficulties in the way of trusting men."

This is no imaginary trouble and is of vital importance. If we cannot deal with this trouble, it really does make the life of faith an impossible and impractical theory. For nearly everything in life comes to us through human means, and most of our trials are the result of somebody's failure, or ignorance, or carelessness, or sin. We know God cannot be the author of these things. Yet, unless He is the agent in the matter, how can we tell Him that we desire His will regarding it?

Besides, what good is there in trusting our affairs

to God if man is to be allowed to come in and disarrange them. How is it possible to live by faith, if human agencies, in whom it would be wrong and foolish to trust, are to have a prevailing influence in molding our lives?

Moreover, things which have God's hand in them always have a sweetness that consoles while it wounds. On the other hand, trials inflicted by man are full of nothing but bitterness.

Receive All As From God

We must see God in everything, and receive everything directly from His hands. We must be brought to this before we can know an abiding experience of entire abandonment and perfect trust. Our abandonment must be to God, not to man. Our trust must be in Him, or we shall fail at the first trial.

Study these scriptures which tell us that we are not to worry about anything because the Father cares for us.

"One (sparrow). . .shall not fall on the ground without your Father. . .the very hairs of (our) head are all numbered" (Matthew 10:29,30).

"Dearly beloved, avenge not yourselves, but rather give place unto wrath: for it is written, Vengeance is Mine; I will repay, saith the Lord" (Romans 12:19).

"We may boldly say, the Lord is my helper, and I will not fear what men shall do unto me" (Hebrews 13:6).

"If God be for us, who can be against us?"

(Romans 8:31).

"The Lord is my shepherd; I shall not want" (Psalm 23:1).

"When thou passest through the waters, I will be with thee; and through the rivers, they shall not overflow thee: when thou walkest through the fire, thou shalt not be burned; neither shall the flame kindle upon thee" (Isaiah 43:2).

"He changeth the times and the seasons: He removeth kings and setteth up kings" (Daniel 2:11).

"(He) bringeth the counsel of the heathen to nought: He maketh the devices of the people of none effect" (Psalm 33:10).

"Hast thou not known? Hast thou not heard, that the everlasting God, the Lord, the Creator of the ends of the earth, fainteth not, neither is weary? There is no searching of His understanding" (Psalm 40:28).

"God is our refuge and strength, a very present help in trouble. Therefore (we will not) fear, though the earth be removed, and though the mountains be carried into the midst of the sea; though the waters thereof roar and be troubled, though the mountains shake with the swelling thereof" (Psalm 46:1,2,3).

"I will say of the Lord, He is my refuge and my fortress: my God; in Him will I trust. Surely He shall deliver thee from the snare of the fowler, and from the noisome pestilence. He shall cover thee with His feathers, and under His wings shalt thou trust: His truth shall be thy shield and buckler.

Thou shalt not be afraid for the terror by night; nor for the arrow that flieth by day; nor for the pestilence that walketh in darkness; nor for the destruction that wasteth at noonday. A thousand shall fall at thy side, and ten thousand at thy right hand; but it shall not come nigh thee. . .Because thou hast made the Lord, which is my refuge, even the most High, thy habitation; there shall no evil befall thee, neither shall any plague come nigh thy dwelling. For He shall give His angels charge over thee, to keep thee in all thy ways'' (Psalm 91:2-7, 9-11).

"Be content with such things as ye have: for He hath said, I will never leave thee, nor forsake thee. So that we may boldly say, the Lord is my helper, and I will not fear what man shall do unto me'' (Hebrews 13:5,6).

To my own mind, these scriptures, and many others like them, settle forever the question regarding the power of "second causes" in the life of the children of God. Second causes must all be under the control of our Father. Not one of them can touch us except with His knowledge and by His permission. No man or company of men, no power in earth or heaven, can touch that soul which is abiding in Christ without first passing through His encircling presence and receiving the seal of His permission.

A Father's Protection

An earthly parent's care for his helpless child is an example of this, although it is a weak example.

If the child is in its father's arms, nothing can touch it without that father's consent, unless he is too weak to prevent it. And even if this should be the case, he first suffers the harm in his own person before he allows it to reach his child. If an earthly parent would care for his little helpless one in this way, how much more will our Heavenly Father care for us, whose love is infinitely greater, and whose strength and wisdom can never be baffled! I am afraid there are even some of God's own children who scarcely think that He is equal to themselves in tenderness, and love, and thoughtful care. In their secret thoughts they charge Him with a neglect and indifference of which they would feel themselves incapable. The truth is that His care is infinitely superior to any human care. He, who counts the very hairs of our heads, and suffers not a sparrow to fall without Him, takes note of the minutest matters that can affect the lives of His children. He regulates them all according to His own perfect will.

There are numerous examples of this. Take Joseph, for instance. What could have seemed to be more utterly contrary to the will of God than the action of his brothers in selling him into slavery? And yet Joseph, in speaking of it, said, "But as for you, ye thought evil against me; but God meant it unto good" (Genesis 50:20). "Now therefore be not grieved, nor angry with yourselves, that ye sold me hither: for God did send me before you to preserve life" (Genesis 45:5).

Joseph's brothers undoubtedly sinned, but by

the time it had reached Joseph it had become God's will for him, and was in truth, though he did not see it then, the greatest blessing of his whole life. And thus we see how God can make even "the wrath of man (to praise Him)" (Psalm 76:10), and how all things, even the sins of others, will work together for good to those that love God.

I learned this lesson long before I knew the scriptural truth concerning it. I was attending a prayer meeting held in the interests of the life of faith, when a lady rose to speak. I looked at her, wondering who she could be, little thinking she was to bring a message to my soul which would teach me a grand practical lesson. She said she had great difficulty in living the life of faith on account of the second causes that seemed to her to control nearly everything that concerned her. Her perplexity became so great that at last she began to ask God to teach her the truth about it, whether He really was in everything or not. After praying this for a few days, she had what she described as a vision. She thought she was in a perfectly dark place. A body of light came toward her from a distance, which gradually surrounded and enveloped her and everything around her. As it approached, a voice seemed to say, "This is the presence of God! This is the presence of God!" While surrounded with this presence, all the great and awful things in life seemed to pass before her—fighting armies, wicked men, raging beasts, storms and pestilences, sin and suffering of every kind.

At first she shrank back in terror. But she soon saw that the presence of God so surrounded and enveloped her and each one of these things, that not a lion could reach out its paw, nor a bullet fly through the air, except as the presence of God moved out of the way to permit it. And she saw that if so thin a film of this glorious Presence were between herself and the most terrible violence, not a hair of her head could be ruffled, nor anything touch her, except as the Presence divided to let the evil through. Then all the small and annoying things of life passed before her. She also saw that she was so enveloped in this presence of God that not a cross look, nor a harsh word, nor petty trial of any kind could affect her unless God's encircling presence moved out of the way to let it.

Her difficulty vanished. Her question was answered forever. God *was* in everything. She saw that clearly. She saw that her life came to her, day by day and hour by hour, directly from the hand of God. Never again did she find any difficulty in an abiding consent to His will and an unwavering trust in His care.

Joy In Trials

If it were only possible to make every Christian see this truth as plainly! I am convinced it is the only way to a completely restful life. Nothing else will enable a soul to live only in the present moment, as we are commanded to do, and to take no thought for the morrow. The Christian will then be able to say, "Surely goodness and mercy shall follow me all the days of my life" (Psalm 23:6). Under God's care we run no risks. I once heard of a poor woman who earned a precarious living by daily labor, but who was a joyous, triumphant Christian. "Ah, Nancy," said a gloomy Christian lady to her one day, who almost disapproved of her constant cheerfulness, and yet envied it—"Ah, Nancy, it is all well enough to be happy now, but I think the thoughts of your future would sober you. Only suppose, for instance, that you would have a spell of sickness, and be unable to work. Suppose your present employers should move away and no one else would give you anything to do. Suppose—" "Stop!" cried Nancy, "I never suppose. The Lord is my Shepherd, and I know I shall not want. And," she added to her gloomy friend, "it is all those 'supposes' that are making you so miserable. You better give them all up and just trust the Lord."

Nothing else but seeing God in everything will make us loving and patient with those who annoy and trouble us. They will then only be the instruments for accomplishing His tender and wise purposes toward us, and we will even find ourselves inwardly thanking them for the blessings they bring.

Nothing else will completely put an end to all murmuring or rebelling thoughts. Christians often feel free to murmur against men when they would not dare murmur against God. If our Father permits a trial to come, we must accept it with thanks from His dear hand. This does not mean, however, that we must like or enjoy the trial itself, but that we must see God's will in the trial. It is not hard to do this, when we have learned to know that His will is the will of love and is, therefore, always lovely.

A very good illustration of this may be found in the familiar fact of a mother giving medicine to her dearly loved child. The bottle holds the medicine, but the mother gives it; and the bottle is not responsible. But, no matter how full her closet may be of bottles or medicine, the mother will not allow one drop to be given to the child unless she believes it will be good for the child. When she does believe it will be good for her darling, the very depth of her love compels her to force it on the child, no matter how bitter the taste.

The people around us are often the bottles that hold our medicine, but it is our Father's hand of love that pours out the medicine and compels us to drink it. The human bottle is the "second cause" of our trial. The medicine that these human "bottles" hold is prescribed for us and given to us by the Great Physician of our souls, who is seeking to heal all our spiritual diseases.

Will we then rebel against the human bottles? Will we not rather take thankfully from our Father's hand the medicine they contain? We must lose sight of the second cause and say joyfully, "Thy will be done, in everything that comes to us, no matter what its source may be."

Seeing our Father in everything makes life one

long thanksgiving and gives a rest of heart. More than that, it gives a joyfulness that cannot be described.

God is sure to have His own way concerning those who abandon themselves to Him in perfect trust. He will lead them into wonderful green pastures of inward rest and beside blessedly still waters of inward refreshment!

He who sides with God cannot fail to win in every encounter. In all circumstances we can join in the Apostle's shout of victory, "Now thanks be unto God, which always causeth us to triumph in Christ" (2 Corinthians 2:14).

Part III

RESULTS

Chapter 13

BONDAGE OR FREEDOM

There are two kinds of Christian experience, one of which is an experience of bondage, and the other an experience of freedom.

In bondage the soul is controlled by a stern sense of duty and obeys the law of God either from fear of punishment or from expectation of wages. In the experience of freedom, the controlling power is an inward life-principle that works out, by the force of its own motions or instincts, the will of the divine Life-giver without fear of punishment or hope of reward. In the first the Christian is a servant and works for hire. In the second he is a son and works for love.

This contrast in the experience of Christians should not be. To "walk in freedom" is plainly their only right and normal condition. But as we have to deal with what is, rather than with what ought to be, we cannot shut our eyes to the sad condition of bondage in which so many of God's children spend a large part of their Christian lives. The reason and the remedy for this are not difficult to find. The reason is legality and the remedy is Christ.

Nowhere do we find those two forms or stages of Christian life more fully developed and contrasted than in the Epistle to the Galatians. The occasion of its being written was that some Jewish brethren came among the churches in Galatia. They tried to draw them away from the liberty of the gospel by presenting certain forms and ceremonies as necessary to their salvation. Peter allowed himself to unite with these teachers. Therefore Paul reproves, not only the Galatians, but also Peter himself.

Neither Peter nor the Galatians committed any moral sin. They did, however, commit a spiritual sin. They got into a wrong attitude toward God—a legal attitude. They began, as Christians generally do, in the right attitude. That is, they entered by the "hearing of faith" into the spiritual life. But when it came to a question of how they were to live in this life, they changed their ground. They sought to substitute works for faith. Having "begun in the Spirit," they were now seeking to be "made perfect by the flesh." They descended in their Christian living from the plane of life to the plane of law.

An illustration will help us to understand this. There are two men who do not steal. Outwardly their actions are equally honest, but inwardly there is a vital difference. One man had a dishonest nature that wants to steal, and is prevented from doing so only by the fear of a penalty. The other possesses an honest nature that hates thieving and could not be induced to steal even by the hope of a reward. The one is honest in the spirit. The other is honest only in the flesh. No words are needed to identify which sort the Christian life is meant to be.

Bondage In Legalism

We are, however, continually tempted to forget that it is not what men *do* that is important, but what they *are*. In Christ Jesus neither following or not following legal observances matters. 2 Corinthians 5:17 tells us, "Therefore if any man be in Christ, he is a new creature: old things are passed away; behold, all things are become new." God is more concerned about our really *being* "new creatures" than about anything else. He knows that if we *are* right in our inward being, we will certainly *do* right in our outward actions. We may, in fact, sometimes even *do* right without *being* right at all. It is very evident that no doing of this kind has any vitality in it, nor is of any real account. The essential thing is character. *Doing* is valuable only as it is an indication of *being*.

Paul was grieved with the Galatian Christians because they seemed to have lost sight of this vital truth—that the inward life, the "new creature," was the only thing that mattered. They began on this plane, but fell from grace to a lower plane. Romans 7:6 tells us, "But now we are delivered from the law. . .we should serve in newness of spirit, and not in the oldness of the letter."

143

"Christ is become of no effect unto you, whosoever of you are justified by the law; ye are fallen from grace" (Galatians 5:4).

This passage is the only one in which the expression "fallen from grace" is used in the New Testament. It means that the Galatians made the mistake of thinking that something else other than Christ was necessary for their right Christian living. The Jewish brethren who had come among them had taught them that Christ alone was not enough, and obedience to the ceremonial law must be added.

They, therefore, believed that some ceremonies of the Jewish ritual were necessary for salvation, and had tried to urge the "Gentiles to live as do the Jews" (Galatians 2:14). Modern Christians are greatly surprised at them and wonder how they could have been so legal. But are not some modern Christians tempted in a different way to follow legality? *They* added the ceremonial law. We add resolutions, or Christian work, or church going, or religious ceremonies of one sort or another. Therefore, what is the difference between us and them? It does not make much difference what you add, the wrong thing is to add anything at all.

We condemn outward deeds and outward ceremonies as bringing salvation. But I fear there are many like the Galatian Christians who frustrate the grace of God by legalism.

The following contrasts may help some to understand the difference between these two beliefs, and may enable them to discover where the secret of their own experience of legal bondage lies:

The Law says:	**The Gospel says:**
Do this and you will live. (See Leviticus 18:5).	*Live*, and then you will do.
Pay what you owe.	God *forgives* you. (See Luke 7:42)
"Make you a new heart and spirit" (Ezekiel 18:31)	"I will *give* them one heart, and I will put a new spirit within you" (Ezekiel 11:19).
"And thou shalt love the Lord God with all thine heart, and with all they soul, and with all thy might" (Deuteronomy 6:5).	"Herein is love, not that we loved God, but that He loved us, and sent His Son to be the propitiation for our sins" (1 John 4:10).
"Cursed be he that confirmeth not all the words if this law to do them" (Deuteronomy 27:26).	"Blessed are they whose iniquities are forgiven, and whose sins are covered" (Romans 4:7).

"The wages of sin is death" (Romans 6:23).

"The gift of God is eternal life through Jesus Christ our Lord" (Romans 6:23).

THE LAW	THE GOSPEL
Demands holiness.	*Gives* holiness.
Says, *Do*.	Says, *Done*.
Extorts the unwilling service of a slave.	*Wins* the loving service of a son.

THE LAW	THE GOSPEL
Makes blessings the result of *obedience*.	Makes obedience the result of *blessings*.
Says, *If*.	Says, *Therefore*.
Was given to restrain man's old nature.	Was given to bring freedom to man's new nature.
Salvation was *wages*.	Salvation is a *gift*.

Christ Set Us Free

Paul tells us that the law is our "schoolmaster" (Galatians 3:25), not our savior. He emphasizes the fact that it is our schoolmaster only for the purpose of bringing us to Christ, for after faith in Christ is come, he declares we are no longer to be under a schoolmaster. He uses the contrast between a servant and a son as an illustration of his meaning in Galatians 4:7. "Wherefore," he says, "thou art no more a servant, but a son." Galatians 5:11 begs us, because of this, to "Stand fast in the liberty wherewith Christ hath made us free, and be not entangled again with the yoke of bondage."

It is as if a woman was paid for her work in weekly wages as a servant in a house. She was under the law of her master, whom she tried to please, but towards whom her service was one only of duty. Finally, however, the master offers her his love, and lifts her up from the place of a servant to be his bride and to share his fortunes. At once the whole spirit of her service is changed. She may perhaps continue to do the same things that she did before, but she does them now from a different motive. The old sense of duty is lost in the new sense of love. The cold word "master" is transformed into the loving word "husband." "And it shall be at that day, saith the Lord, that thou shalt call me Ishi (my husband), and shalt call me no more Baali (my lord)" (Hosea 2:16).

But imagine this bride beginning after a while to look back upon her former low position and begin to feel unworthy of union with her husband. Who can doubt that very soon the old sense of working for wages would drive out the new sense of working for love, and in spirit the old name of "my master" would again take the place of the new name of "my husband?"

We are amazed at such thinking. But isn't this just what happens to many Christians now? The slavery of duty takes the place of the service of love. God is looked upon as the stern task-master who demands our obedience, instead of the loving Father who wins it.

We all know that nothing so destroys the sweetness of any relationship as when this legal spirit creeps in. The moment a husband and wife stop serving each other out of a heart of love and union, and begin to serve from a sense of duty alone, the sweetness of the union is lost. The marriage tie then becomes a bondage, and things that were a joy before are turned into crosses.

Many Christians think that taking up the cross means doing something we ought to do, but dislike to do. Such service is thought to have merit. We all know very well that we would not endure it a moment toward ourselves. What wife could endure her husband using language toward her that Christians are continually using toward the Lord? If he would say, for instance, every morning as he went to work, "I am going to work for you today, but I want you to know that it is a very great cross and I hardly know how to bear it." Or what husband would like such language from his wife? No wonder Paul was alarmed when he found there was danger of a legal spirit such as this creeping into the Church of Christ.

Legal Christians do not deny Christ. They only seek to add something to Christ. Their idea is, Christ and—something besides. Perhaps it is

Christ and good works, or Christ and earnest feelings, or Christ and clear doctrines, or Christ and certain religious performances. All these are good in themselves, and good as the results or fruits of salvation. However, to add anything to Christ, no matter how good it may be is to deny His completeness and to exalt self.

A religion of bondage always exalts self. It is what I do—*my* efforts, *my* wrestlings, *my* faithfulness. But a religion of liberty leaves self nothing to glory in; it is all Christ, and what He does, and what He is, and how wonderfully He saves. The child does not boast of itself, but of his father and mother. Our souls can "make (their) boast in the Lord" (Psalm 34:2) when, in this life of liberty, we have learned to know that He and He alone is the sufficient supply for our every need.

Heirs Of God

We are the children of God. Therefore, we are His heirs. Our possessions come to us, not by working for them, but by inheritance from our Father. Ah, dear friends, how little some of you act like the "heirs of God" (Romans 8:17)! How poverty-stricken you are, and how hard you work for the little you do possess!

You may think that good has come from your own effort, which does seem to have a "(show) of wisdom in will worship, and humility, and neglecting of the body" (Colossians 2:23). But I am convinced that any good results have come in spite of, and not because of, your legal working.

149

I had a friend once whose Christian life was a life of bondage. She worked for her salvation harder than any slave ever worked to purchase his freedom. She never felt as if the day could go right for herself or any of her family, unless she started it with a season of wrestling, and agonizing, and conflict. "Winding up her machine," I called it. One day we were talking about it, and she was telling me of the difficulty and bondage of her Christian life. She wondered what the Bible meant when it said Christ's yoke was easy and His burden light (Matthew 11:30). I told her that I thought she must have gotten things wrong somehow, that the Bible did not suggest that any such wrestling and agonizing are necessary.

"What would you think," I asked, "of children who had to wrestle and agonize with their parents every morning for their necessary food and clothing, or of sheep that had to wrestle with their shepherd, before they could secure the necessary care?"

"Of course I see that would be all wrong," she said. "But then why do I have such good times after I have gone through these conflicts?"

This puzzled me for a moment, but then I asked, "What finally brings about those good times?"

"Why, finally," she replied, "I come to the point of trusting the Lord."

"Suppose you came to that point in the beginning?" I asked.

"Oh," she replied, with sudden illumination, "I never until this minute thought that I might!"

Christ says that except we "become as little children" we cannot enter into the Kingdom of heaven (see Matthew 18:3). But it is impossible to get the child-spirit until the servant-spirit has disappeared. Notice, I do not say the spirit of service, but the servant-spirit. Every good child is filled with the spirit of service, but shouldn't have the servant-spirit. The child serves from love. The servant works for wages.

If a child of loving parents would get the idea that its parents would not give him food and clothing unless he earned them in some way, all the sweetness of the relationship between parent and child would be destroyed. I knew a little girl who did get this idea, and who went around the neighborhood asking at the doors for work so that she might earn a little money to buy herself some clothes. It nearly broke the hearts of her parents when they discovered it. Legal Christians grieve the heart of their Heavenly Father, far more than they know, by letting the servant-spirit creep into their relationship with Him. As soon as we begin to "work for our living" in spiritual things, we have stepped out of the son's place into the servant's, and have fallen from grace.

Spiritual Blessings

One servant, of whom we read in the twenty-fifth chapter of Matthew, thought his lord was a hard master. The spirit of bondage makes us think the same now. How many Christians there are who have bowed their necks to the yoke of Christ as to a "yoke of bondage." They have read His declaration that His yoke is easy, as though it were a fairy tale, and gone on their way, never dreaming that it was meant to be actually realized as fact! When some children of God find themselves experiencing freedom, they at once begin to think there must be something wrong in their experience because they no longer find anything to be a "cross" to them. A wife might as well think that there must be something wrong in her love for her husband, when she finds all her services for him are a pleasure instead of a trial!

Sometimes I think that the whole secret of the Christian life that I have been trying to describe is revealed in the child relationship. Nothing more is needed than just to believe that God is as good a Father as the best ideal earthly father. The relationship of a Christian to Him is just the same as that of a child to its parent in this world. Children do not need to carry money with them for their support. If the father has plenty, that satisfies them. This is a great deal better than if it were in the child's own possession since it might get lost. In the same way it is not necessary for Christians to have all their spiritual possessions in their own keeping. It is far better that their riches should be stored up for them in Christ, and that when they want anything they should receive it directly from His hands. Christ is "made unto us wisdom, and righteousness, and sanctification, and redemption" (1 Corinthians 1:30). Apart from Him, we have nothing.

When people are comparative strangers to one another, they cannot receive gifts from each other comfortably. But when they are united in spirit with a bond of true love between them, no matter how great the gifts, they can be accepted without embarrassment or obligation.

This principle holds true in the spiritual life. When Christians are living apart from God, they cannot be brought to accept any great gifts from Him. They feel as if they are too unworthy and do not deserve such gifts. Even when He puts the blessing into their hands, their false humility prevents them from seeing it, and they go on their way without it.

But when Christians get near enough to the Lord to feel the true spirit of adoption, they are ready to accept with delight all the blessings He has in store for them. They never think anything is too much to receive. For then they discover that He is only eager, as parents are, to pour out every good gift upon His children. All things are theirs because they are Christ's, and Christ is God's.

Bondage Or Freedom

Sometimes a great mystery is made out of the life hid with Christ in God, as though it were a strange mystical thing that ordinary people could not understand. But this contrast between bondage and freedom makes it very plain. It is only to find out that we really are sons, not servants (see Galatians 4:7), that we can enter into the blessed privileges of this relationship. All can understand what

153

it is to be a little child. There is no mystery about that. God did not use the description of Father and children without knowing all that this relationship implies. Those who know Him as their Father know the whole secret. They are their Father's heirs and may enter now into possession of all that is necessary for their present needs. They will therefore be very simple in their prayers. "Lord," they will say, "I am your child, and I need such and such." "My child," He answers, "all things are yours in Christ. Come and take just what you need."

Where the executors of an estate are honorable men, the heirs are not obliged to "wrestle" for their inheritance. The executors are appointed to help them possess it. I sometimes think Christians look upon our Lord as someone appointed to keep them out of their possessions, instead of the one who has come to bring them in. They know little how such an implication grieves and dishonors Him.

It is because legal Christians do not know the truth of their relationship to God, as children to a father, and do not recognize His fatherly heart toward them, that they are in bondage. When they do recognize it, the spirit of bondage becomes impossible to them.

Our freedom must come, therefore, from an understanding of the mind and thoughts of God towards us.

What are the facts of the case? If He has called us to the servants' place, rather than the Christians',

154

whose lives are lives of weary bondage, we are right. But if He has called us to be children and heirs, if we are His friends, His brethren, His bride, how sadly and grievously wrong we are in being entangled under any yoke of bondage whatever, no matter how pious a yoke it may seem to be!

The thought of bondage is utterly abhorrent to any of earth's true relationships, and surely it must be more repugnant to a heavenly relationship. It will not hinder the final entrance of the poor enslaved soul into its heavenly rest, but it will put it into the sad condition of those who are described in 1 Corinthians 3:11-15. "(Their) work shall be burned, (and they) shall suffer loss; (yet they themselves) shall be saved; yet so as by fire."

"Against such there is no law" (Galatians 5:23) is the divine sentence concerning all who live and walk in the Spirit. You will find it most blessedly true in your own experience, if you will lay aside all self-effort and self-dependence of every kind, and will consent to let Christ live in you, work in you, and be your indwelling life.

The man who lives by the power of an inward righteous nature is not under bondage to the outward law of righteousness. But, he who is restrained by the outward law alone, without the inward restraint of a righteous nature, is a slave to the law. The one fulfills the law in his soul, and is therefore free. The other rebels against the law in his soul, and is therefore bound.

I truly wish that every child of God knew the deliverance from bondage which I have tried to present!

Chapter 14

GROWTH

A great objection made against those who promote this life of faith is that they do not teach growing in grace. According to them, the soul arrives in one moment at a state of perfection which cannot advance. All the scriptures that point toward growth and development are ignored by this teaching.

I want to present what Scripture says about growth. I also want to discuss the condition the soul must be in so that growth can take place.

The text most frequently quoted is 2 Peter 3:18: "But grow in grace, and in the knowledge of our Lord and Savior Jesus Christ." Now, this text expresses exactly what we who teach this life of faith believe to be God's will for us and what He has made possible for us to experience. We fully accept all the commands and promises concerning our growing up into Christ in all things, until we come "unto a perfect man unto the measure of the stature of the fullness of Christ" (Ephesians 4:13). We rejoice that we do not have to continue being babes in Christ, only needing milk. We rejoice that we can develop into needing strong meat, skillful in the word of righteousness and able to discern good and evil. No one would grieve more than we at the thought of a Christian life with no advancement.

We believe in a growth that continually produces maturity. We believe in a development that brings forth ripe fruit. We expect to reach the aim set before us. If we do not find ourselves heading toward it, we feel sure there must be something wrong in our "growing". No parent would be satisfied with the growth of his child if day after day and year after year he remained the same helpless babe he was in the first months of his life. And no farmer would feel comfortable if his grain would stop short at the blade and never produce the ear or the full corn in the ear.

To be real, growth must be progressive. The days and weeks and months should bring an increase of maturity in the thing growing. But is this the case with a large part of what is called growth in grace? Doesn't the Christian who most longs and works after this growth find, too often, that he has not come far in his Christian experience? He often recognizes that his zeal, his devotedness, and his separation from the world are not as definite or complete as when his Christian life first began.

Grow In Grace

I was once urging a group of Christians in the

duty and privilege of an immediate and definite step into the "land of promise," when a lady of great intelligence interrupted me with what she evidently felt to be a complete rebuttal of all I had been saying. She exclaimed, "Ah! but, Mrs. Smith, I believe in *growing* in grace."

"How long have *you* been growing?" I asked.

"About twenty-five years," was her answer.

"And how much more unworldly and devoted to the Lord are you now, than when your Christian life began?" I continued.

She answered, "I am afraid not very much." And with this answer her eyes were opened to see that her way of growing had not been successful.

The trouble with her and with others like her is simply this: they are trying to grow *into* grace, instead of *in* it. The children of Israel, wandering in the wilderness, are a perfect picture of this sort of growing. They were traveling for forty years, taking many weary steps, and finding little rest from their wanderings. Yet, at the end of it all, they were no nearer the promised land than they were at the beginning. When they started on their wanderings at Kadesh Barnea, they were at the borders of the land, and a few steps would have taken them into it. When they ended their wanderings in the plains of Moab, they were also at its borders. However, now there was a river to cross. All their wanderings and struggles in the wilderness did not put them in possession of one inch of the promised land. In order to get possession of this land, it was necessary first to be in it. In order to grow in grace, it is first necessary to be planted in grace. When once in the land the Israelites' conquest was rapid. When once planted in grace, the growth of the spiritual life becomes vigorous and rapid beyond all thinking. For grace is a most fruitful soil, and the plants that grow therein are plants of a marvelous growth. They are tended by a divine Husbandman and are warmed by the Sun of Righteousness, and watered by the dew from heaven. Surely it is no wonder that they bring forth fruit, "some an hundred-fold, some sixty-fold, some thirty-fold" (Matthew 13:8).

What is meant by growing in grace? It is difficult to answer this question because so few people have any conception of what the grace of God really is. To say that it is free unmerited favor only expresses a little of its meaning. It is the unhindered, wondrous, boundless love of God, poured out upon us in an infinite variety of ways without measure. Although we do not deserve it, grace comes from His measureless heart of love.

I sometimes think an entirely different meaning is given to the word "love" when it is associated with God. We seem to think that divine love is different and self-seeking and distant, concerned about its own glory, and indifferent to the fate of others. But if human love was ever tender, self-sacrificing, and devoted, it would suffer gladly for its loved one. It would willingly pour itself out in lavish abandonment for the comfort or pleasure of its object. However, divine love is then infinitely more tender, self-sacrificing, and devoted. It is eager to lavish its best of gifts and blessings upon the objects of its love. Put together all the tenderest love you know, the deepest and strongest you have ever felt, heap upon it all the love of all the loving human hearts in the world, multiply it by infinity, and you will begin perhaps to have some faint glimpses of the love and grace of God!

In order to "grow in grace," the soul must be planted in the very heart of this divine love, enveloped by it, steeped in it. The soul must give itself to the joy of it, and must refuse to know anything else. Day by day the soul must entrust everything to the care of this divine love and must not doubt that all will be well ordered.

Growth Without Anxiety

Growth in grace is opposed to growth by self-effort or legality of every kind. It is to put our growing, as well as everything else, into the hands of the Lord, and leave it with Him. It is to be so satisfied with our Husbandman and with His skill and wisdom, that not a question will cross our minds concerning His methods of treatment and cultivation. It is to grow as the lilies grow, or as the babies grow, without care and without anxiety. He who has planted us, has made us to grow.

Surely this is what our Lord meant when He said, "Consider the lilies of the field, how they grow; they toil not, neither do they spin: And yet I say unto you, that even Solomon in all his glory was not arrayed like one of these" (Matthew 6:28,29). Or, when He says in Matthew 6:27,

"Which of you by taking thought can add one cubit unto his stature?" There is no effort in the growing of a baby or of a lily. The lily doesn't toil or spin, it doesn't stretch or strain, it doesn't make any effort to grow, it is not even conscious that it is growing. But through the nurturing care of God, the care of the gardener, the heat of the sun, and the falling of the rain, it grows and buds and blossoms into the beautiful plant God meant it to be.

The result of this sort of growing in the Christian life is sure. "Even Solomon in all His glory," our Lord says, "was not arrayed like one of (God's lilies)." Solomon's clothing cost much in work and money. However, though we may work hard trying to make beautiful spiritual garments for ourselves, and though we may work hard in our efforts to gain spiritual growth, we shall accomplish nothing. For no man by taking thought can add one cubit to his stature, and no array of ours can ever equal the beautiful dress with which the great Husbandman clothes the plants that grow in His garden of grace and under His fostering care.

If I could make each of my readers realize how utterly helpless we are in this matter of growing, I am convinced a large part of the strain would be taken out of many lives at once.

Imagine a child possessed of the worry that he would not grow unless he made some personal effort to do so. Suppose he tried to use a combination of ropes and pulleys to stretch himself up to the desired height. He might, it is true, spend his days and years in a weary strain. There would be no changing the fact that "No man by taking thought can add one cubit unto his stature." His weary efforts would be only wasted, and might even actually hinder the long-awaited end.

Neither a child nor a lily is ever found doing such a vain and foolish thing as *trying* to grow. But I fear many of God's children are doing exactly this foolish thing. They know that they ought to grow, and they feel within them an instinct that longs for growth. But instead of letting the divine Husbandman care for their growing, as it is surely His business to do, they try to accomplish it themselves. Consequently, they waste their energies and find themselves not growing at all.

What we all need is to "consider the lilies of the field" and learn their secret. Grow, by all means, dear Christians, but grow in God's way. See to it that you are planted in grace, and then let the divine Husbandman cultivate you in His own way and by His own means. Put yourselves out in the sunshine of His presence and let the dew of heaven come down upon you. See what the results will be. Leaves and flowers and fruit must come in their season, for your Husbandman is skillfull and He never fails in His harvesting. Only see to it that you do not hinder the shining of the Sun of Righteousness, or the falling of the dew from heaven. The thinnest covering may serve to keep off the sunshine and the dew, causing the plant to wither. So the slightest barrier between your soul and Christ may cause you to dwindle and fade as a plant in a cellar or under a bush. Keep the sky clear. Receive the blessed influences your divine Husbandman may bring to bear upon you. Bask in the sunshine of His love. Drink of the waters of His goodness. Keep your face upturned to Him as the flowers do to the sun. Look, and your soul will live and grow.

Abide In The Vine

Someone may be thinking that, after all, we are not inanimate flowers but intelligent human beings with personal powers and personal responsibilities. This is true. The important difference is that what the flower is by nature, we must be by an intelligent and free surrender. To be one of God's lilies means an interior abandonment of the rarest kind. It means that we are to be infinitely passive and infinitely active also. We are to be passive regarding self, and we are to be active regarding our attention and response to God. It is very hard to explain this and be understood. But it means that we must lay down all the activity of the creature and must let only the activities of God work in us, through us, and by us. Self must step aside to let God work.

Therefore, you do not have to make any effort to grow, but let your efforts concentrate on this— that you abide in the Vine. The divine Husbandman who has the care of the Vine will care also for you who are His branches. He will prune and purge and water and tend you, so that you will grow and bring forth fruit. Your fruit will remain, and like the lily, you will find yourself arrayed so glorious that Solomon's apparel will be nothing compared with it.

What if you seem to be planted at this moment in a desert soil, where nothing can grow! Put yourselves completely into the hands of the good Husbandman, and He will begin at once to make the desert blossom as the rose. He will cause springs and fountains of water to start up out of its sandy wastes. For the promise is sure, that the man that trusts in the Lord "shall be as a tree planted by the waters, and that spreadeth out her roots by the river, and shall not see when heat cometh, but her leaf shall be green; and shall not be careful in the year of drought, neither shall cease from yielding fruit" (Jeremiah 17:8).

It is the great prerogative of our divine Husbandman that He is able to turn any soil, whatever it may be like, into the soil of grace, the moment we put our growing into His hands. He does not need to transplant us into a different field. Right where we are, with just the circumstances that surround us, He makes His sun to shine and His dew to fall upon us. He transforms the very things that were our greatest hindrances to the most blessed means of our growth. I don't care what the circumstances may be, His wonder-working power can accomplish this. We must trust Him with it all. We can trust. And if He sends storms, or winds, or rains, or sunshine, all must be accepted at His hands with the most unwavering confidence that He, who has undertaken to cultivate us and to bring us to maturity, knows the very best way of accomplishing His end.

Let yourselves grow. Leave it all to the care and management of the Husbandman. No difficulties in your case can baffle Him. If you will only put yourselves completely into His hands, and let Him have His own way with you, nothing in your past life can mar the perfect work that He will accomplish. His own gracious promise to His backsliding children assures you of this. In Hosea 14:4-7 He says, "I will heal their backsliding. I will love them freely: for Mine anger is turned away from him. I will be as the dew unto Israel: he shall grow as the lily, and cast forth his roots as Lebanon. His branches shall spread, and his beauty shall be as the olive-tree, and his smell as Lebanon. They that dwell under His shadow shall return; they shall revive as the corn, and grow as the vine: the scent thereof shall be as the wine of Lebanon." And again He says: "Be not afraid. . .for the pastures of the wilderness do spring, for the tree beareth her fruit, the fig-tree and the vine do yield their strength. . .And the floors shall be full of wheat, and the vats shall overflow with wine and oil. And I will restore to you the years that the locust hath eaten. . . .And ye shall eat in plenty, and be satisfied, and praise the name of the Lord your God, that hath dealt wondrously with you: and My people shall never be ashamed" (Joel 2:22-26).

Contentment In Growth

Oh that you could know just what your Lord

meant when He said, "Consider the lilies of the field, how they grow; they toil not, neither do they spin." Surely these words give us the picture of a life and growth far different from the ordinary life and growth of Christians—a life of rest and a growth without effort. Yet, a life and a growth crowned with glorious results. We may be assured that all the resources of God's infinite grace will be brought to bear on the growing of the tiniest flower in His spiritual garden as certainly as they are in His earthly creation. As the violet abides peacefully in its little place, content to receive its daily portion without concerning itself about the wandering of the winds, or the falling of the rain, so must we rest in the present moment as it comes to us from God. We must be contented with our daily portion, without anxious thought as to anything that may be whirling around us in God's glorious universe, sure that all things will be made to "prosper" for us.

This is the kind of "growth in grace" in which we who have entered into the life of full trust, believe—a growth without care or anxiety. A growth which does actually grow, which blossoms out into flower and fruit, and becomes like a "tree planted by the rivers of water, that bringeth forth his fruit in his season; his leaf also shall not wither, and whatsoever he doeth shall prosper" (Psalms 1:3). And we rejoice to know that there are growing up now in the Lord many such plants who are "beholding as in a glass the glory of the Lord (being changed) into the same image from glory to glory, even as by the Spirit of the Lord" (2 Corinthians 3:18).

They grow so rapidly and with such success because they are not concerned about their growing and are hardly conscious that they do grow. It is enough for them that their Lord has told them to abide in Him and has promised that if they do abide in Him, they will certainly bring forth much fruit. They are only concerned with their part—abiding. They are content to leave the cultivating, growing, training, pruning, to their good Husbandman, who alone is able to manage these things. You will find that such souls are not engaged in watching self, but in "looking unto Jesus" (Hebrews 12:2). They do not "toil and spin" for their spiritual garments, but leave themselves in the hands of the Lord to be arrayed as it may please Him. Formerly they tried to be not only the garden but the gardener as well, and tried to fulfill the duties of both. Now they are content to *be* what they *are*—the garden only, and not the gardener. They are willing to leave the gardener's duties to the divine Husbandman. Their interest in self is gone, transferred over into the hands of another. Christ alone is seen to be all in all.

Let us look at the subject practically. We all know that growing is not a thing of effort, but is the result of an inward life-principle of growth. All the stretching and pulling in the world could not make a dead oak grow. A live oak grows without stretching. It is plain that the essential thing is to get within you the growing life, and then you cannot help but grow. And this life is the "life hid with Christ in God," the wonderful divine life of an indwelling Holy Spirit. Be filled with this, dear believer, and whether you are conscious of it or not, you *must* grow, you cannot help growing. Do not trouble about your growing, but see to it that you have the growing life. Abide in the Vine. Yield yourself up utterly to His lovely control. Put your growing into His hands as completely as you have put all your other affairs. Do not concern yourself about it. Do not even think it. Do not, as children do, keep digging up your plants to see if they are growing. Trust the divine Husbandman absolutely and always. Accept each moment as it comes to you from His dear hands, as being the needed sunshine or dew for that moment's growth. Say a continual "Yes" to your Father's will. And finally, in this, as in all the other cares of your life, "Be careful for nothing; but in everything, by prayer and supplication with thanksgiving let your requests be made known unto God. And the peace of God that passeth all understanding shall keep your hearts and minds through Christ Jesus" (Philippians 4:6,7).

If your "growth in grace" is of this sort, you will surely know, sooner or later, a wonderful growing. You will come to understand what the Psalmist meant when he said, "The righteous shall flourish like the palm-tree: he shall grow like a cedar in Lebanon. Those that be planted in the house of the Lord shall flourish in the courts of our God. They shall bring forth fruit in old age; they shall be fat

and flourishing'' (Psalm 92:12-14).

Chapter 15

SERVICE

Upon entering this life hid with Christ in God, there is, perhaps, no part of Christian experience where a greater change is known than in the matter of service.

In all the ordinary forms of Christian life, service is more or less a type of bondage in that it is done purely as a matter of duty and often as a trial and a cross. Certain things, which at first may have been a joy and a delight, become weary tasks. These tasks may be performed faithfully, without a great desire to do them. The soul finds itself saying, instead of the "May I?" of love, the "Must I?" of duty. The yoke which was at first easy, begins to irritate, and the burden feels heavy instead of light.

One dear Christian expressed it once to me in this way: "When I was first converted," she said, "I was so full of joy and love, that I was only too glad and thankful to be allowed to do anything for my Lord, and I eagerly entered every open door. But after a while, as my early joy faded away, and my love burned less fervently, I began to wish I had not been quite so eager. I found myself involved in areas of service that were gradually becoming very distasteful and burdensome to me. Since I had begun them, I could not very well give them up without causing comment, and yet I longed to do so increasingly. I was expected to visit the sick, and pray beside their beds. I was expected to attend prayer meetings, and speak at them. I was expected, in short, to be always ready for every effort in Christian work, and the sense of these expectations bowed me down continually. At last it became so unspeakably burdensome to me to live the sort of Christian life I had entered upon, and was expected by all around me to live, that I felt as if any kind of manual labor would have been easier. I would have infinitely preferred scrubbing all day on my hands and knees to being compelled to go through the treadmill of my daily Christian work. I envied," she said, "the women in the kitchen."

Some may think this to be a strong statement, but does it not present a vivid picture of some of your own experiences? Have you never gone to work as a slave to his daily task, believing it to be your duty and that you must do it, but later returning to your real interests and pleasures the moment your work was over?

You have known that this was the wrong way to feel, and have been thoroughly ashamed of it, but still you have seen no way to help it. You have not *loved* your work. If you could have done so with an easy conscience, you would have been glad to give it up altogether.

Or, if this doesn't describe your case, perhaps another example will. You do love your work, but in doing it you find so many cares and responsibilities connected with it and feel so many misgivings and doubts as to your own capacity or fitness that it becomes a very heavy burden. You go to it bowed down and weary, before the labor has even begun. Also, you are continually distressing yourself about the results of your work, and you are greatly troubled if they are not just what you would like. This of itself is a constant burden.

Serving In Love

The soul that fully enters into the blessed life of faith is entirely delivered from all these forms of bondage. Service of any sort becomes delightful to the soul. Having surrendered the will into the Lord's keeping, the Lord works in it to will and to do of His good pleasure, and the soul finds itself really *wanting* to do the thing God wants it to do. It is always very pleasant to do the things we *want* to do no matter how difficult they are or how tired we get from doing them.

If a man's *will* is really set on doing something, he is indifferent to the obstacles that lie in the way of his reaching it. He laughs to himself at the idea of any opposition or difficulties hindering him. How many men have gone gladly and thankfully to the ends of the world in search of worldly fortunes, or to fulfill worldly ambitions, and have scorned the thought of any "cross" connected with it! How many mothers have congratulated themselves, and rejoiced over the honor done their sons in seeing them promoted to some place of power and usefulness in their country's service, although it has involved perhaps years of separation and a life of hardship for their dear ones! And yet these same men and mothers would have felt and said that they were taking up crosses too heavy almost to be borne had the service of Christ required the same sacrifice of home, friends, and worldly ease.

It is altogether the way we look at things, whether we think they are crosses or not. And I am ashamed to think that any Christian should ever put on a long face and shed tears over doing something for Christ which a worldly man would be only too glad to do for money.

What we need in the Christian life is to get believers to *want* to do God's will as much as other people want to do their own will. This is the idea of the Gospel. It is what God intended for us. It is what He has promised. In describing the new covenant in Hebrews 8:6-13, He says it will no longer be the old covenant made on Sinai—that is, a law given from the outside, controlling a man by force. But the new covenant will be a law written *within*, constraining a man by love. "I will put my laws," He says, "into their mind, and write them in their hearts." This can mean nothing but that we will *love* His law for anything written in our hearts we must love. "And putting it into our minds" is surely the same as God working in us to "will and to do of His good pleasure." This means that we will desire what God wills and shall obey His sweet commands, not because it is our duty to do so, but because we ourselves want to do what He wants us to do.

Nothing could possibly be better than this. How often have we thought, when dealing with our children, "Oh, if I could only get inside of them and make them *want* to do just what I want, how easy it would be to manage them then!" How often in practical experience, when dealing with difficult people, we carefully avoid suggesting our wishes to them, and must in some way cause them to suggest the thing themselves so that there will be no opposition. We are a stubborn people who rebel against something if someone else presents the idea to us, while we would think it to be an excellent idea if we had thought of it ourselves.

God's way of working is to get possession of the inside of a man, to take the control and management of his will, and to work it for Him. Then obedience is easy and a delight, and service becomes perfect freedom.

If you are in bondage in the matter of service you need to put your will completely into the Lord's hands, surrendering to Him the entire control of it. Say, "Yes, Lord, *yes!*" to everything. Trust Him to work in you to bring your whole wishes and affections into conformity with His own sweet lovable, and most lovely will. I have seen this done often, in cases where it looked to be impossible.

In one case, where a lady had been rebelling fearfully for years against an act of service which she knew was right but which she hated, I saw her, out of the depths of despair and without any feeling, give her will in that matter up into the Lord's hands. She said to Him, "Thy will be done. *Thy will be done!*" And in one short hour that very thing began to look sweet and precious to her.

Strength In Yielding

It is wonderful what miracles God works in wills that are utterly surrendered to Him. He turns hard things into easy things and bitter things into sweet things. It is not that He puts easy things in the place of the hard, but He actually changes the hard thing into an easy one and makes us love to do the thing we hated. When we rebel against the yoke and try to avoid it, we are bitter about it and find it difficult. But when we take the yoke upon us with a consenting will, we find it easy and comfortable. It is said of Ephraim that at one time he was like "a bullock unaccustomed to the yoke" (Jeremiah 31:18). But afterwards, when he had submitted to the yoke, he was "as an heifer that is taught, and loveth to tread out the corn" (Hosea 10:11).

Many Christians, as I have said, love God's will generally, but carry great burdens in connection with it. There is deliverance from this in the wonderful life of faith. For in this life no burdens are carried, no anxieties felt. The Lord is our Burden-bearer, and we must give Him every care. He says, in effect, "Be careful for nothing, but. . .(make) your request known. . .to Me, and I will attend to them all" (Philippians 4:6). Be careful for *nothing,* He says, not even your service. Above all, our service would not amount to anything because we know ourselves to be utterly helpless in regard to it, even if we were careful.

Why should we think about whether we are fit or not? The Master-workman surely has a right to use any tool He pleases for His own work, and it is plainly not the business of the tool to decide whether it is the right one to be used or not. He knows, and if He chooses to use us, of course we must be fit. In truth, our chief fitness is in our utter helplessness. His strength is made perfect, not in our strength, but in our weakness. Our strength is only a hindrance.

I was once visiting an institution for the handicapped and saw the children exercising with weights. Now, we know that it is a very difficult thing for the handicapped to manage their movements. They generally have strength enough, but have no skill to use this strength. Consequently, they cannot do much. This deficiency was very apparent in these exercises. They made all sorts of awkward movements. Now and then, by chance, they would make a movement in harmony with the music and the teacher's directions, but for the most part all was out of harmony. However, I noticed one little girl who made perfect movements. And the reason was, not that she had more strength than the others, but that she had no strength at all. She could not so much as close her hands over the weights or lift her arms. The teacher had to stand behind her and do it all. She yielded up her members as instruments to him, and his "strength was made perfect" (2 Corinthians 12:9) in her weakness. He knew how to go through those exercises, for he had planned them. Therefore, when he did it, it was done right. She did nothing but yield herself up completely into his hands, and he did it all. The yielding was her part. The responsibility was all his. It was not her skill that was needed to make harmonious movements, but only his. The question doesn't deal with her capacity, but with his. Her total weakness was her greatest strength.

This is a very striking picture of our Christian life, and it is no wonder that Paul could say, "most gladly therefore will I rather glory in my infirmities, that the power of Christ may rest upon me" (2 Corinthians 12:9). Who would not glory in being so utterly weak and helpless, that the Lord Jesus Christ should find no hindrance to the perfect working of His mighty power through us and in us?

Responsibility And Result

Then, too, if the work is His, the responsibility is His also, and we have no room left for worrying about results. He knows everything in reference to it. He can manage it all. Leave it all with Him. It is a fact that the most effectual workers I know are those who do not feel the least care or anxiety about their work, but who commit it all to the Lord. They ask Him to guide them moment by moment in reference to it. They trust Him implicitly for each moment's needed supplies of wisdom and of strength. To look at them, you would almost think that they were too free from care, where such mighty interests are at stake. But when you have learned God's secret of trusting, and see the beauty and the power of the life that is yielded up to His working, you will cease to condemn. You will then begin to wonder how any of God's workers can dare to carry the burdens, or assume the responsibilities, which He alone is able to bear.

Some may object that the Apostle Paul spoke of the "care of all the Churches" (2 Corinthians 11:28) coming upon him. But we must not fail to remember that it was the constant habit of the Apostle to roll every care off on the Lord, and thus, while full of care, to be "without carefulness."

There are one or two other bonds in service from which this life of trust delivers us. We find out that no one individual is responsible for all the work in the world, but only for a small share. Our duty ceases to be universal, and becomes personal and individual. The Master does not say to us, "Go and do everything," but He marks out a special path for each one of us and gives each one of us a special duty. There are "diversities of gifts" (1 Corinthians 12:4) in the Kingdom of God, and these gifts are divided to "every man according to his several ability" (Matthew 25:15). I may have five talents or two or only one. I may be called to do twenty things or one thing. My responsibility is simply to do that which I am called to do, and nothing more. "The steps of a good man are ordered by the Lord" (Psalm 37:23), not his way only, but each separate step in that way.

Many Christians make the further mistake of looking upon every act of service as a perpetual obligation. They think because it was right for them to give a tract to one person in a railway train, for instance, that they are always to give tracts to everybody. In this way they burden themselves with an impossible duty.

There was a young Christian once who, because she had been sent to witness to one soul whom she met in a walk, supposed it was a perpetual obligation. Thus she thought she must witness to every one she met in her walks. Of course this was impossible, and she was in hopeless bondage about it. She became absolutely afraid to step outside of her own door and lived in perpetual condemnation. At last she confided her distress to a friend, who was instructed in the ways of God with His servants. This friend told her she was making a great mistake. The Lord had His own special work for each special workman. The servants in a well-regulated household might as well take it upon themselves to try to do the work of all the rest, as for each of the Lord's servants to think he or she was under obligation to do everything. He told her just to put herself under the Lord's personal guidance regarding her work and trust Him to point out each person to whom He would have her speak. He assured her that the Lord never sends forth His own sheep without going before them and making a way for them Himself. She followed this advice and laid the burden of her work on the Lord. The result was a happy pathway of daily guidance in which she was led into much blessed work for her Master. She was able to do it all without a care or a burden because He led her out and prepared the way before her.

Rest In Service

I have been much instructed myself by thinking of the arrangements of our own households. When we appoint a person for a special part of the work of the household, we want him to attend to that alone, and not run all over the house trying to attend to the work of all the other people. It would make endless confusion in any earthly household if the workers were to act in this fashion, and it makes no less confusion in the divine household.

Our part in the matter of service seems to me just like making the junction between the machinery and the steam engine. The power is not in the machinery, but in the steam. Disconnected from the engine, the machinery is perfectly useless. But make the connection and the machinery goes easily and without effort because of the mighty power behind it. Thus the Christian life, when it is the development of the divine life working within, becomes an easy and natural life. Most Christians live a strained life. Because their wills are not fully in harmony with the will of God, the connection is not perfectly made at every point. It thus requires an effort to move the machinery. But when the connection is fully made and the "law of the Spirit of life in Christ Jesus" can work in us with all its mighty power, we are then indeed made "free from the law of sin and death" (Romans 8:2). They will know the glorious freedom of the children of God.

The life of faith delivers the soul from another form of bondage. It is reference to these thoughts which always follow any Christian work. These thoughts are of two kinds. The soul either congratulates itself upon its success and is lifted up, or it is distressed over its failure and is utterly cast down. One of these is *sure* to come. It is my belief that the first one is to be more dreaded, although the second causes greater suffering at the time. But in the life of trust neither will trouble us. Having committed ourselves in our work to the Lord, we will be satisfied to leave it to Him and not think about ourselves in the matter at all.

Years ago I came across this sentence in an old book: "Never indulge, at the close of an action, in any self-reflective acts of any kind, whether of self-congratulation or of self-despair. Forget the things that are behind, the moment they are past, leaving them with God." This has been of unspeakable value to me. When the temptation to reflect comes, I turn from the thoughts at once and positively refuse to think about my work at all. Rather, I leave it with the Lord to overrule the mistakes and to bless it as He chooses. I believe there would be far fewer "blue Mondays" for ministers of the Gospel than there are now, if they would adopt this plan. And I am sure all workers would find their work far less tiresome.

To sum it all up, then, what is needed for happy and effective service is simply to put your work into the Lord's hands and leave it there. Do not take it to Him in prayer, saying, "Lord, guide me. Lord, give me wisdom. Lord, arrange for me," and then rise from your knees, take the burden all back, and try to guide and arrange for yourself. *Leave* it with the Lord. Remember that what you trust to Him you must not worry nor feel anxious about. Trust and worry cannot go together. If your work is a burden, it is because you are not trusting it to Him. But if you do trust it to Him, you will surely find that the yoke He puts upon you is easy and the burden He gives you to carry is light. Even in the midst of a life of ceaseless activity, you will "find rest unto your souls" (Matthew 11:29).

If the divine Master only had a band of workers like this, there would be no limit to what He might do with them. Truly, one such worker would "chase a thousand, and two would put ten thousand to flight" (Deuteronomy 32:30). And nothing would be impossible to them. For it is nothing with the Lord "to help, whether with many, or with them that have no power" (2 Chronicles 14:11). If only He can find instruments that are fully given to His working.

May God raise up such an army speedily! And may you, my dear reader, enroll your name among this band. Yielding yourself unto God as one who is "alive from the dead" (Romans 6:13), may every one of your members also be yielded to Him as "instruments of righteousness" (Romans 6:13) to be used by Him as He pleases!

Chapter 16

PRACTICAL RESULTS IN THE DAILY WALK

If all that has been written in the preceding chapters on the life hid with Christ is true, its results ought to be very noticeable in our daily walk as Christians. The people who have entered into the enjoyment of it ought to be "peculiar people, zealous of good works" (Titus 2:14).

My son once wrote to a friend saying something to this effect: that we are God's witnesses necessarily, because the world will not read the Bible, but they will read our lives. Their belief in the divine nature of the faith we possess will be influenced by our lives. This age is essentially an age of facts. All scientific inquiries are being increasingly turned from theories to realities. If Christianity is to make any headway in the present time, it must be proved to be more than a theory. We must present to the investigation of the critical minds of our age the realities of lives transformed by the mighty power of God.

I want to speak very solemnly concerning what I see to be the necessary fruits of a life of faith such as I have been describing. I want to convince every one of my readers about their personal responsibility to walk "worthy of this calling" (2 Thessalonians 1:11).

I think that I may speak to some of you as personal friends. I am sure I will be pardoned if I go into some details of our daily lives which may seem of lesser importance, but which make up the largest part of our existence.

A Christlike Nature

The standard of practical, holy living has been so low among Christians that the least degree of real devotedness of the higher Christian walk is looked upon with surprise and often even with disapproval by a large portion of the Church. For the most part, the followers of the Lord Jesus Christ are satisfied with a life so conformed to the world in almost every respect that, to a causal observer, no difference is discernible.

But we, who have heard God call us to a life of entire consecration and perfect trust, must do differently. We must come out from the world and be separate. We must not be conformed to it in our characters or in our lives. We must set our affections on heavenly things, not on earthly ones. We must first seek the Kingdom of God and His righteousness and surrender everything that would interfere with this. We must walk through the world as Christ walked. We must have the mind that was in Him. As pilgrims and strangers, we must abstain from fleshly lusts that war against the soul. As good soldiers of Jesus Christ, we must disentangle ourselves inwardly from the affairs of this life, that we may please Him who has chosen us to be soldiers. We must abstain from all appearance of evil. We must be kind to one another, tenderhearted, forgiving one another, even as God, for Christ's sake, has forgiven us. We must not resent injuries or unkindness, but must return good for evil, and turn the other cheek to the hand that hits us. We must always take the lowest place among our fellow-men. We must not seek our own honor, but the honor of others. We must be gentle, meek, and yielding. We must not stand up for our own rights, but for the rights of others. We must do everything, not for our own glory, but for the glory of God. And, to sum it all up, since He who has called us is holy, so we must be holy in all manner of conversation. It is written, "be holy, for I am holy" (Leviticus 11:45).

Some Christians seem to think that all the requirements of a holy life are met when there is very active and successful Christian work. Because they do so much for the Lord in public, they feel a liberty to be cross and ugly and un-Christlike in private. But this is not the sort of Christian life I am depicting. If we are to walk as Christ walked, it must be in private as well as in public, at home as well as abroad. It must be every hour all day long, and not at stated periods or on certain fixed occasions. We must be Christlike everywhere and to all. It is in daily living that practical holiness can best show itself, and we may well question any "professions" that fail under this test of daily life.

An anxious Christian, a discouraged, gloomy Christian, a doubting Christian, a complaining Christian, an exacting Christian, a selfish Christian, a cruel, hard-hearted Christian, a self-indulgent Christian, a Christian with a sharp tongue or bitter spirit, may be a very earnest worker and have an honorable place in the Church. But, he or she is *not* a Christlike Christian, and knows nothing of the lessons of this book concerning the higher Christian life.

People must see that we walk as Christ walked, if we say that we are abiding in Him. We must prove that we "possess" that which we "profess." We must, in short, be real followers of Christ, not followers in theory only. This means a great deal. It means that we must completely turn our backs on everything that is contrary to the perfect will of God. It means that we are to be a "peculiar people" (Titus 2:14), not only in the eyes of God, but in the eyes of the world around us. Wherever we go, it should be known from our habits, our attitudes, our conversation, and our pursuits, that we are followers of the Lord Jesus Christ. We must demonstrate that we are not of the world, even as He was not of the world. We must no longer look upon our money as our own. We must look at it as belonging to the Lord to be used in His service. We must not feel at liberty to use our energies exclusively in the pursuit of worldly means, but must recognize: "seek ye first the kingdom of God, and His righteousness; and all these things shall be added unto you" (Matthew 6:33). We will find ourselves forbidden to seek the highest places or to strain after worldly advantages. We will not be permitted to make self the center of all our thoughts and all our aims. Our days will have to be spent, not in serving ourselves, but in serving the Lord. We will find ourselves called upon to bear one another's burdens and so fulfill the law of Christ. All our daily duties will be performed more perfectly than ever because whatever we do will be done, "Not with eye-service, as men-pleasers; but as the servants of Christ, doing the will of God from the heart" (Ephesians 6:6).

Results Of A Hidden Life

We will undoubtedly be led into all this by the Spirit of God, if we give ourselves up to His guidance. But unless we have the right standard of Christian life set before us, we may be hindered from recognizing His voice by our ignorance. I desire to be very plain and definite in my statements for this reason.

I have noticed that wherever someone has been truly faithful following the Lord, several things have inevitably followed sooner or later. Meekness and quietness of spirit in time become the characteristics of the daily life. A submissive acceptance of the will of God is shown as it comes in the hourly events of each day. There is a willingness in the believer whose life is in the hands of God to do or to suffer all the good pleasure of His will. There is a sweetness when provoked. There is a calmness in the midst of turmoil. There is a yielding to the wishes of others, and an insensibility to slights and affronts. There is absence of worry or anxiety. There is deliverance from care and fear. All these, and many other similar graces, are invariably found to be the natural, outward development of that inward life which is hid with Christ in God.

We see such Christians sooner or later laying aside thoughts of self and becoming full of consideration for others. They dress and live in simple, healthful ways. They renounce self-indulgent habits and surrender all purely fleshly gratifications. Some helpful work for others is taken up, and useless occupations are dropped out of the life. God's glory, and the welfare of His creatures, become the absorbing delight of the soul. The voice is dedicated to Him, to be used in singing His praises. Money is placed at His disposal. The pen is dedicated to write for Him. The lips are dedicated to speak for Him. The hands and the feet are dedicated to do His bidding. Year after year such Christians are seen to grow more unworldly, serene, heavenly-minded, transformed, and more like Christ, until even their faces express so much of the beautiful, inward, divine life, that all who look at them can see that they live with Jesus. They are abiding in Him.

Have you not begun to feel dimly conscious of the voice of God speaking to you in the depths of your soul about these things? Has it not been painful and distressing to discover how full your lives are of self? Has your soul been plunged into inward trouble and doubt about certain attitudes or desires in which you have formerly indulged? Have you begun to feel uneasy with some of your habits of life? Have you wished that you could do differently? Haven't paths of dedication and service begun to open out before you with the longing thought, "Oh, that I could walk in them!"?

Moment By Moment Obedience

All these questions and doubts and this inward yearning are the voice of the Good Shepherd in your heart, seeking to call you out of that which is contrary to His will. I beg you not to turn away from His gentle pleadings! You know little about the sweet paths into which He means to lead you by these very steps. You know little of the wonderful stores of blessings that lie at their end, or you would spring forward with an eager joy to yield to every one of His requirements.

The heights of Christian perfection can only be reached each moment by faithfully following the Guide who is to lead you there. He reveals the way to us one step at a time, in the little things of our daily lives, asking only that we yield ourselves up to His guidance. Be perfectly pliable then in His dear hand. Go where He leads you. Turn away from all which He causes you to shrink from. Obey Him perfectly the moment you are sure of His will and you will soon find that He is leading you out swiftly and easily into such a wonderful life of conformity to Himself. It will be a testimony to all around you, beyond what you could have ever thought.

I knew a soul dedicated in this way to follow the Lord wherever He might lead her. She went from the depths of darkness and despair into the realization and actual experience of a most blessed union with the Lord Jesus Christ. Out of the midst of her darkness she consecrated herself to the Lord. She surrendered her will completely to Him so that He might work in her to will and to do His own good pleasure. Immediately He began to speak to her by His Spirit in her heart, suggesting to her some little act of service for Him, and troubling her about certain things in her habits and her life. He showed her where she was selfish and un-Christlike, and how she could be transformed. She recognized His voice and yielded to Him each thing He asked for, the moment she was sure of His will. Her swift obedience was rewarded by a rapid progress. Day by day she was conformed more and more to the image of Christ. Her life became such a testimony to those around her that some who had begun by opposing and disbelieving were forced to acknowledge that it was of God and were won to a similar surrender. And finally, her Lord was able to reveal to her wondering soul some of the deepest secrets of His love, by fulfilling the marvelous promise of Acts 1:5—by giving her the baptism of the Holy Spirit. Do you think she has ever regretted her wholehearted following of Him? Do you think that anything but thankfulness and joy can ever fill her soul when she reviews the steps by which her feet have been led to this place of wondrous blessing? It is divine joy even though some of those steps may have seemed at the time hard to take. Ah, dear soul, if you would like a similar blessing, abandon yourself like her, to the guidance of your divine Master, and shrink from no surrender for which He may call.

Surely you can trust Him! And if you think that something may not be worthy of the Lord's attention, remember that He does not see as man sees, and things that seem small to you may be the key and the clue to the deepest springs of your being in His eyes. No life can be complete that fails in its little things. However small a look, a word, even a tone of voice may seem to human judgment, they are often of vital importance in the eyes of God. Your one great desire is to follow Him fully. Can you not continually say, "Yes" to all His sweet commands, whether they are small or great? Trust Him to lead you by the shortest road to your fullest blessedness.

My dear friend, whether you know it or not, this, and nothing less than this, is what consecration means. It means inevitable obedience. It means that the will of God is to be your will, under all circumstances and at all times. It means that you surrender your freedom of choice, and give yourself up completely into the control of the Lord. It means following Him hourly, wherever He might lead you, without any turning back.

All this and far more was involved in your surrender to God, and now I appeal to you to make good your word. Let everything else go, that you may live in a practical, daily walk and conversation, the Christ-life you have dwelling within you. You are united to the Lord by a wondrous tie. Walk, then, as He walked, and show to the unbelieving world the blessed reality of His mighty power to save, by letting Him save you to the very uttermost. Do not fear to consent to this, for He is your Savior, and His power is to do it all. He is not asking you to do it yourself. He only asks that you yield yourself up to Him, that He may work in you and through you by His own mighty power.

Your part is to yield yourself. His part is to work. Never, never will He give you any command that is not accompanied by ample power to obey it. Take no thought for the future in this matter. Abandon yourself with a generous trust to the Good Shepherd, who has promised never to call His own sheep out into any path without going before them to make the way easy and safe. Take each little step as He makes it plain to you. Let Him regulate and guide all the details of your life. Follow the sweet suggestions of His Spirit in your soul gladly and quickly. And day by day you will find Him bringing you more and more into conformity with His will in all things, molding and fashioning you as you are able to bear it, into a "vessel unto honor, sanctified and meet for the master's use, and prepared unto every good work" (2 Timothy 2:21). Your light will shine so brightly, that men seeing, not you, but your good works, will glorify, not you, but your Father which is in heaven.

195

Chapter 17

THE JOY OF OBEDIENCE

Having spoken of some of the difficulties in this life of faith, let me now speak of some of its joys. The joy of obedience is foremost.

Long ago I came across this sentence: "Perfect obedience would be perfect happiness, if only we had perfect confidence in the power we were obeying." I remember being struck with the saying as the means of a possible, though undreamed of, way of happiness. I thought of that saying often, even when full of inner rebellion. It gave me the vision of a rest—and yet a vision of a possible development—that would soothe and at the same time satisfy all my yearnings.

Need I say that this rest has now been revealed to me, not as a vision, but as a reality. I have seen the Lord Jesus as the way to perfect rest when we yield to Him and take His yoke upon us.

Dear hesitating soul, you are missing such joy! The Master has revealed Himself to you and is calling for your complete surrender. Yet, you withdraw and hesitate. You are partially willing, and you think it is fit and proper that you should feel thus. But a complete surrender, without any reserve, seems to you to be too much. You are afraid of it. You think it involves too much and is too great a risk.

Then, too, you see other souls who seem able to walk with easy consciences in a far wider path than that which appears to be marked out for you, and you ask yourself why this is so. It seems strange that you must do what they do not have to do, and must avoid what they feel free to do.

Surrender Without Limitation

Dear Christian, this very difference between you is your privilege, though you do not yet know it. Your Lord says, "He that hath My commandments, and keepeth them, he it is that loveth Me; and he that loveth Me shall be loved of My Father, and I will love him, and will manifest myself to him." You *have* His commandments. Those you envy do not have them. *You* know the mind of your Lord about many things. Those walking in darkness do not. Is this not a privilege? Should you regret that your soul is in such close relationship with your Master that He is able to tell you things which those less close may not know? Do you not realize the tender degree of intimacy in this?

There are many relationships in life that require little devotion. We may have pleasant friendships with one another, and yet spend a large part of our lives in separate interests and goals. When together, we may greatly enjoy one another's company, but when we are separated we are upset or anxious. There is not enough love between the two parties to give either the right or the desire to enter into and share each other's most private affairs. A certain degree of reserve and distance seems to be the suitable thing in this kind of relationship, but there are other relationships in life where all this is changed. The friendship becomes love. The two hearts give themselves to each other, to no longer be two, but one. A union of soul takes place, which makes all that belongs to one the property of the other. Separate interests and separate paths in life are no longer possible. Things that were acceptable before become unacceptable now, because of the nearness of the tie that binds. The reserve and distance suitable to mere friendship becomes fatal in love. Love gives all and must have all in return. The wishes of one become binding obligations to the other, and the deepest desire of each heart is that it may know every secret wish or longing of the other, in order that it may gratify it.

When this kind of love relationship exists the people involved do not complain of the yoke. They do not envy the cool, calm, reasonable friendships they see around them. They do not regret the closeness which this kind of love requires or the obligations it creates. Rather, they glory in these obligations and inwardly pity the ones who do not have such a relationship! Every fresh revelation of the wishes of the loved one is a fresh delight and privilege. No path is considered too hard for them to travel.

If you have ever known this, even for a few hours in an earthly relationship, if you have ever loved any of your fellow human beings enough to find sacrifice and service on their behalf a joy, do so also with your divine Savior. If a complete surrender of your will to the will of another has ever been a blessed and longed-for privilege, then, by all the tender, longing love of your heavenly Master, I beg you to let it be so toward Christ!

He loves you with more than the love of friendship. He has given you all, and He asks for all in return. The slightest reserve will grieve Him to the heart. He did not spare Himself. How can you spare yourself? For your sake He completely surrendered all that He had, and for His sake you must surrender all that you have, without limitation or measure.

Oh, be generous in your self-surrender! Meet His measureless devotion for you with a measureless devotion to Him. Be glad and eager to throw yourself completely into His loving arms and to hand over the reins of government to Him. Whatever there is of you, let Him have it all. Give up forever everything that is separate from Him. Consent to give up, from this time forward, all freedom of choice. Glory in the close relationship with Jesus which makes this enthusiasm of devotedness not only possible, but necessary.

Separated Unto Him

Have you ever longed to lavish your love and

attentions on someone who is unapproachable or who is a stranger? Have you ever strongly wanted to be surrendered and devoted to someone? Will you shrink or hesitate if you hear the loving voice of your Lord calling you into a place of nearness that will require a separation from all else and will make an enthusiastic devotion not only possible, but necessary? Will you think it harsh that He reveals to you more of His mind than He does to others and that He will not allow you to be happy in anything that separates you from Himself? Do you *want* to go where He cannot go with you, or to have desires which He cannot share?

A thousand times no! You will meet His lovely will with an eager joy. Even His slightest wish will become a binding law to you and it will break your heart to disobey it. You will glory in the paths He marks out for you and will grieve for the ones who have missed this precious joy. The obligations of love will be sweetest privileges. Surrendering all that you have to the Lord will seem to lift you into a region of unspeakable glory. The perfect happiness of perfect obedience will dawn upon your soul, and you will begin to know something of what Jesus meant when He said, "I delight to do Thy will, O My God."

But do you think that the only joy in this will be yours? Has the Lord no joy in those who have surrendered themselves to Him and who love to obey Him? My friends, we are not able to understand this, but the Scriptures reveal glimpses of the delight, the satisfaction, the joy our Lord has in us.

It is easy to understand that we need Him, but it is hard to believe that He should need us. And yet He says it, and what can we do but believe Him? He has made our hearts capable of this affection and has offered Himself as the object of it. It is infinitely precious to Him. He values it so much that He has made it the first and most important of all His commandments. We are to love Him with all our might and with all our strength. He is knocking at every heart, asking to be taken in as the supreme object of love. "Will you let Me be your Beloved? Will you follow Me into suffering and loneliness and endure hardship for My sake? Will you ask for no reward except My smile of approval and My word of praise? Will you surrender to My will? Will you give Me total control of yourself and of all that you have? Will you be content with pleasing Me and Me only? May I have My way with you in all things? Will you separate yourself from the world? Will you accept Me for your heavenly Bridegroom and leave all others to cleave only unto Me?" He makes this offer to every believer in a thousand ways. But all do not say "Yes" to Him. Other loves and other interests seem too precious to be cast aside. They do not miss heaven because of this, but they miss an unspeakable present joy.

You, however, are not one of these. From the very first your soul has cried out eagerly and gladly to all His offers, "Yes, Lord, yes!" You are more than ready to pour out all your richest treasures of love and devotion to Him. You have surrendered to Him with such enthusiasm that it may disturb and distress some moderate Christians. Your love makes a separation from the world necessary. A lesser love cannot even understand this. It is with love that you sacrifice for and serve your loved ones. The life of love gives you the right to lavish your *all* upon your beloved One. Your Lord claims far more from you because of your union with Him. He makes His secrets known to you. He looks for an instant response to every requirement of His love.

Let Him Have All

It is altogether wonderful. It will not matter to you if men hate you and separate themselves from you. It will not matter to you if men condemn you. If this happens for His sake, Scripture says your reward is great in heaven for if you are a partaker of His suffering, you will also be a partaker of His glory.

Your love and devotion are His precious reward for all He has done for you. It is unspeakably sweet to Him. Do not be afraid, then, to let yourself go in wholehearted devotion to the Lord. Others may not approve, but He will. That is enough. Do not be stingy with your obedience or your service. Let your heart and your hand be as free to serve Him as His heart and hand were to serve you. Let Him have all there is of you: body, soul, mind, spirit, time, talents, voice, everything. Lay your whole life open before Him so that He may control it. Say each day to Him, "Lord, enable me to regulate this day to please You! Give me spiritual insight to discover what Your will is in all the relationships of my life. Guide me regarding my desires, my friendships, my reading, my dress, my Christian work." Do not let a day or an hour go by in which you are not consciously doing His will and following Him completely.

Such a personal service to your Lord will enrich the poorest life and give the most monotonous existence a heavenly glow. Have you ever grieved that the romance of youth is so soon lost in the hard realities of the world? Bring Christ into your life and into all its details, and a romance—far grander than the brightest days youth could ever know—will thrill your soul, and nothing will seem difficult or unbearable again.

When Christ was on earth, He declared the truth that there was no blessedness equal to the blessedness of obedience. "And it came to pass, as He spake these things, a certain woman of the company lifted up her voice, and said unto Him, Blessed is the womb that bare Thee, and the paps which Thou hast sucked. But He said, Yea rather, blessed are they that hear the word of God, and keep it" (Luke 11:27-28).

It is more blessed to hear and obey His will than even to have been the earthly mother of our Lord!

May our surrendered hearts reach out with an eager delight to discover and embrace the lovely will of our loving God!

Chapter 18

DIVINE UNION

All the dealings God has with the soul of the believer are to bring it into oneness with Himself, that the prayer of our Lord may be fulfilled: "That they all may be one; as Thou, Father, art in Me, and I in Thee, that they also may be one in us. . . .I in them, and Thou in Me, that they may be made perfect in one; and that the world may know that Thou hast sent Me, and hast loved them, as Thou hast loved Me" (John 17:21,23).

This divine union was the glorious purpose in the heart of God for His people before the foundation of the world. It was the mystery hidden from ages and generations. It was accomplished in the death of Christ. It has been made known by the Scriptures. It is realized as an actual experience by many of God's dear children.

However, it is not experienced by all. God has not hidden this union or made it hard, but the eyes of many are too dim and their hearts too unbelieving for them to grasp it. It is for the purpose of bringing His people into the personal and actual realization of this that the Lord calls upon them so earnestly and so repeatedly to abandon themselves to Him. Thus He may work in them all the good pleasure of His will.

All the previous steps in the Christian life lead up to this. The Lord has made us for it, and, until we have understood it, and, have voluntarily consented to embrace it, the "travail of His soul" (Isaiah 53:11) for us is not satisfied, nor have our hearts found their destined and real rest.

The Reality Of The Christlife

The usual course of Christian experience is pictured in the history of the disciples. First, they were awakened to see their condition and their need and came to Christ and gave their allegiance to Him. Then they followed Him, worked for Him, believed in Him, yet how unlike Him they were— seeking to be set up one above the other. They were running away from the cross, misunderstanding His mission and His words. They were forsaking their Lord in time of danger. But still they were sent out to preach, recognized by Him as His disciples, possessing power to work for Him. They knew Christ as their Lord and Master, but did not yet know Him as their life.

Then came Pentecost and these same disciples came to know Him as one with them in actual union, their very indwelling life. From then on they knew what He was within them, working in them to will and to do of His good pleasure, delivering them, by the law of the Spirit of His life, from the bondage to the law of sin and death under which they had been held. No longer did their wills and interests war with Him. His will alone motivated them. His interest alone was dear to them. They were made *one* with Him.

Surely all can recognize this picture, though perhaps the final stage of it has not yet been fully reached. You may have given up much to follow Christ. You may have believed on Him and worked for Him and loved Him, and yet may not be like Him. Allegiance you know, and confidence you know, but you do not yet know union. There are two wills, two interests, two lives. You have not yet lost your own life that you may live only in His. Once it was "I and not Christ." Next it was "I and Christ." Perhaps now it is even "Christ and I." But has it yet come to be Christ only, and not I at all?

If you have followed me through all the previous chapters in this book, you will surely now be ready to take the definite step of faith which will lead your soul out of self and into Christ. You will then be prepared to abide in Him forever and to know no life but His.

You only need to understand what the Scriptures teach about this marvelous union and see that it is intended for you.

Read 1 Corinthians 3:16, "Know ye not that ye are the temple of God, and that the Spirit of God dwelleth in you," and then look at the opening of the chapter to see who these wonderful words are spoken to: even to "babes in Christ" who were "yet carnal" and walked according to men. You will then see that this soul-union of which I speak, this unspeakably glorious mystery of an indwelling God, is the possession of even the weakest and most failing believer in Christ. It is true that every believer's "body is the temple of the Holy Ghost, which is in you, which ye have of God" (1 Corinthians 6:19).

But although this is true, it is also equally true that the believer has to know it and live in the power of it. Like the treasures under a man's field which existed there before they were known or used by him, so does the life of Christ dwell in each believer before he knows it and lives in it. Its power is not manifested until, intelligently and voluntarily, the believer ceases from his own life and accepts Christ's life in its place.

But it is very important not to make any mistakes here. This union with Christ is not a matter of emotions, but of character. It is not something we are to *feel*, but something we are to *be*. The vital thing is not the feeling, but the reality.

Living In Our Emotions

No one can be one with Christ who is not Christlike. This is a manifest truth. Yet, it is often overlooked. Often very strong emotions of love and joy are taken as signs and proofs of divine union in cases where essential proofs of a Christlike life and character are lacking. This is completely contrary to the Scripture declaration that "He that saith he abideth in Him ought himself also to walk, even as He walked" (1 John 2:6). There is no escape from this, for it is not only a divine declaration, but is in the very nature of things as well.

We speak of being one with a friend and we mean that we have a union of purposes and thoughts and desires. No matter how enthusiastic our friends may be in their expressions of love and unity, there can be no real oneness between us unless there are, at least in some degree, the same likes, dislikes, thoughts, purposes, and ideals. Oneness with Christ means being made a "partaker of (His) nature" (2 Peter 1:4) as well as of His life, for nature and life are, of course, one.

If we are really one with Christ, it will not be contrary to our nature to be Christlike and to walk as He walked, but it will be in accordance with our nature. Sweetness, gentleness, meekness, patience, long-suffering, charity, and kindness will all be natural to the Christian who is a partaker of the nature of Christ. It could not be otherwise.

But people who live in their emotions do not always see this. They *feel* so at one with Christ that they look no farther than this feeling. They often delude themselves by thinking they have come into the divine union, when all the while their nature and dispositions are still under the sway of self-love.

Our emotions are most untrustworthy and are largely the result of our physical condition or our natural temperaments. It is a fatal mistake, therefore, to make them the test of our oneness with

Christ. This mistake works both ways. If I have very joyous emotions, I may be deluded by thinking I have entered into the divine union when I have not. If I have no emotions, I may grieve over my failure to enter into the divine union when I really have entered.

Character is the only real test. God is holy and those who are one with Him will be holy also. Our Lord Himself expressed His oneness with the Father in such words as these: "The Son can do nothing of Himself, but what He seeth the Father do: for what things soever He doeth, these also doeth the Son likewise" (John 5:19). "If I do not the works of My Father, believe Me not. But if I do, though ye believe not Me, believe the works; that ye may know, and believe, that the Father is in Me, and I in Him" (John 10:37-38).

The test Christ gave, by which the reality of His oneness with the Father was to be known, was the fact that He did the works of the Father. I know of no other test for us now.

It is forever true in the nature of things that a tree is to be known by its fruits. If we have entered into the divine union we will bear the divine fruits of a Christlike life and conversation: for "He that saith, I know Him, and keepeth not His commandments, is a liar, and the truth is not in him. But whoso keepeth His word, in him verily is the love of God perfected: hereby know we that we are in Him" (1 John 2:4-5).

Pay no regard to your feelings in this matter of oneness with Christ, but see to it that you have the really vital fruits of a oneness in character and walk and mind. Your emotions may be very delightful, or they may be very depressing. In neither case are they any real indication of your spiritual state. Very undeveloped Christians often have very powerful emotional experiences. I knew one who was kept awake often by the "waves of salvation," as she expressed it, which swept over her all night long. But she did not yet tell the truth in her conversation with others, and was very far from honest in her business dealings. No one could possibly believe that she knew anything about a real, divine union, in spite of all her fervent emotions in regard to it.

Your joy in the Lord is to be a far deeper thing than a mere emotion. It is to be the joy of knowledge, of perception, of actual existence. It is a far better thing to *be* a bird, with all the actual realities of flying, than only to *feel* as if you were a bird, with no actual power of flying at all. Reality is always the vital thing.

Awareness Of Christ's Presence

But now, having guarded against this danger of an emotional experience of divine union, let us consider how the reality is to be reached. First I would say that it is not a new attitude to be taken by God, but only a new attitude to be taken by us. If I am really a child of God, then my heart is already the temple of God and Christ is already within me. What is needed, therefore, is only that I recognize His presence and yield fully to His

211

control.

It is as though Christ were living in a house, shut up in a far-off closet, unknown and unnoticed by the dwellers in the house, longing to make Himself known to them and to be one with them in all their daily lives and share in all their interests. But He is unwilling to force Himself upon their notice because nothing but a voluntary companionship could meet or satisfy the needs of His love. The days pass by and those of the household remain ignorant about their marvelous privilege. They go about all their daily affairs with no thought of their wonderful Guest. Their plans are laid without reference to Him. His wisdom to guide and His strength to protect are all lost to them. Lonely days and weeks are spent in sadness which might have been full of the sweetness of His presence.

But suddenly the announcement is made, "The Lord is in the house!" How will its owner receive the knowledge? Will he call out an eager thanksgiving and throw every door wide open for the entrance of his glorious Guest? Or will he withdraw and hesitate, afraid of His presence, and seek some private corner for a refuge from His all-seeing eye?

Dear friend, I tell you the Lord is in your heart. Since the day of your conversion He has been dwelling there, but you have lived in ignorance of it. During all that time, every moment might have been passed in the sunshine of His sweet presence and every step taken under His advice. But because you did not know it and did not look for Him there, your life has been lonely and full of failure. But now that I make you aware of this, how are you going to receive it? Are you glad to have Him? Will you throw every door wide open to welcome Him in? Will you joyfully and thankfully give up your life to Him? Will you consult Him about everything and let Him decide each step and mark out every path? Will you invite Him into your innermost chambers and share your most hidden life with Him? Will you say "Yes" to His longing for union with you? Will you, with a glad and eager surrender, hand yourself and all that concerns you over into His hands? If you will do this your soul will begin to know something of the joy of union with Christ.

A Voluntary Invitation

But words fail me here! All that I can say cannot describe the blessed reality. It is far more glorious to be brought into a real and actual union with Him and be one with Him—one will, purpose, interest, life—than it would be to have Christ as a dweller in the house or in the heart. Human words cannot express such a glory as this. And yet it ought to be expressed and our souls ought to be made so hungry for it, that day or night we should not be able to rest without it. Do you understand what it means to be one with Christ? Do you catch the slightest glimpse of the meaning? Does your whole soul begin to exult over such a wondrous destiny? It seems too wonderful to be true that such poor, weak, foolish beings like us should be created for such an end as this. Yet it is a blessed reality. We are even *commanded* to enter into it. We are exhorted to lay down our lives so that His life may be lived in us. We are asked to have no interests but His interests, to share His riches, to enter into His joys, to partake of His sorrows, to have the same mind as He had, and to think and feel and act and walk as He did.

Will we agree to all this? The Lord will not force it on us because He wants us as His companions and His friends, and a forced union would be incompatible with this. It must be voluntary on our part. The bride must say a willing "Yes" to the bridegroom, or the joy of their union is in question. Can we say a willing "Yes" to our Lord?

It is a very simple transaction and yet very real. There are three steps. First, we must be convinced that the Scriptures teach this glorious indwelling of God. Then we must surrender our whole selves to Him to be possessed by Him. And finally, we must believe that He *has* taken possession and *is* dwelling in us. We must begin to consider ourselves dead and to consider Christ as our only life. We must maintain this attitude of soul unwaveringly. It will help us to say, "I am crucified with Christ: nevertheless I live; yet not I, but Christ liveth in me" (Galatians 2:20) over and over, day and night, until it becomes the habitual breathing of our souls. We must continually deny self and put on the life of Christ.

We must do this, not only by faith, but practically as well. We must continually put self to death in all the details of daily life and must let Christ live and work in us instead. We must never do the selfish thing, but always the Christlike thing. We must let this become, by its constant repetition, the attitude of our whole being. And as we do this we will understand at last something of what it means to be made one with Christ as He and the Father are one. Christ left all to be joined to us. We must also leave everything to be joined to Him in this divine union which words cannot express, but for which our Lord prayed when He said, "Neither pray I for these alone, but for them also which shall believe on Me through their word: that they all may be one; as Thou, Father, art in Me, and I in Thee, that they also may be one in us." ·

Chapter 19

THE CHARIOTS OF GOD

It has been well said that "earthly cares are a heavenly discipline." However, they are even something better than discipline—they are God's chariots, sent to take the soul to its high places of triumph.

They do not look like chariots. Instead, they look like enemies, sufferings, trials, defeats, misunderstandings, disappointments, unkindnesses. They look like misery and wretchedness waiting to roll over us and crush us into the earth. But if could we see them as they really are, we would recognize them as chariots of triumph in which we may ride to those heights of victory for which our souls have been longing and praying. The difficulty is the visible thing. The chariot of God is the invisible. The King of Syria came up against Elisha with horses and chariots that could be seen by every eye, but God had chariots that could be seen by none except the eye of faith. The servant of the Prophet could only see the outward and visible. In 2 Kings 6:15 he cried, "Alas, my Master! how shall we do?" But Elisha sat calmly within his house without fear, because his eyes were opened to see the invisible. All he asked for his servant was, "Lord, I pray Thee open his eyes that he may see" (2 Kings 6:17).

This is the prayer we need to pray for ourselves and for one another, "Lord, open our eyes that we may see." The world all around us, as well as around the Prophet, is full of God's horses and chariots waiting to carry us to places of glorious victory. And when our eyes are opened, we will see in all the events of life, whether great or small, whether joyful or sad, a "chariot" for our souls.

God's Chariots

Everything that comes to us becomes a chariot the moment we treat it as such. And on the other hand, even the smallest trials may crush us into misery or despair if we let them. It is up to us to choose which it will be. It does not matter what these events are, but how we take them. We can either lie down under them and let them roll over us and crush us, or we can view them as chariots of God and make them carry us triumphantly onward and upward.

Whenever we climb into God's chariots the same thing happens to us spiritually that happened to Elijah. We will have a translation, not into the heaven above us as Elijah did, but into the heaven within us. This, after all, is almost a grander translation than his. We will be carried away from the low, earthly, grovelling plane of

217

life, where everything hurts and everything is unhappy, up into the "heavenly places in Christ Jesus" (Ephesians 1:3). There we can ride in triumph over all below.

These "heavenly places" are interior, not exterior. The road that leads to them is interior also. But the chariot that carries the soul over this road is generally some outward loss or trial or disappointment, something that is not joyous, but grievous. However, afterwards it "yieldeth the peaceable fruit of righteousness unto them which are exercised thereby" (Hebrews 12:11).

Our "chariot" often looks very unlovely. It may be a nasty relative or friend. It may be the result of human malice or cruelty or neglect. But every chariot sent by God is paved with love, since God is love. And God's love is the sweetest, softest, tenderest thing that was ever found by any soul anywhere.

The Bible tells us that when God went forth for the salvation of His people He "didst ride upon (His) horses and chariots of salvation" (Habakkuk 3:8) and it is the same now. Everything becomes a "chariot of salvation" when God rides upon it. He "maketh the clouds His chariot" (Psalm 104:3), we are told, and rides "on the wings of the wind" (Psalm 18:10). Therefore, the clouds and storms that darken our skies and seem to shut out the shining of the sun of righteousness are really only God's chariots which we may "ride prosperously" (Psalm 45:4) over all the darkness. Have you made the clouds in your life your chariots? Are you "riding prosperously'' with God on top of them all?

I knew a lady who had a housekeeper who worked slowly. She was an excellent girl in every other respect, and very valuable in the household. However, her slowness was a constant source of irritation to her employer who was naturally quick and who always became irritated at slowness. This lady would lose her temper with the girl twenty times a day, and twenty times a day would repent of her anger and be determined to conquer it, but in vain. Her life was made miserable by the conflict. One day it occurred to her that she had been praying a long while for patience, and that perhaps this slow housekeeper was the very chariot the Lord had sent to carry her soul over into patience. She immediately accepted it as such, and from that time used the slowness of her housekeeper as a chariot for her soul. The result was a victory of patience that no one was ever able to disturb.

I knew another lady at a crowded convention who had to sleep in a room with two others because of the crowd. *She* wanted to sleep, but *they* wanted to talk. The first night she was greatly disturbed and lay there fretting and fuming long after the others had stopped talking, when she might have slept. But the next day she heard something about God's chariots, and at night she accepted these talking friends as her chariots to carry her over into sweetness and patience, and was kept in undisturbed calm. When, however, it grew very late, and she knew they all ought to be sleeping, she ventured to say slyly, "Friends, I am lying here riding in a chariot!" The effect was instantaneous and perfect quiet reigned! Her chariot had carried her over to victory, not only inwardly, but at last outwardly as well.

If we would ride in God's chariots, instead of our own, we would find this to be the case continually.

Earthly Chariots

Our constant temptation is to trust in earthly resources. We can *see* them. They are tangible and real, and look substantial, while God's chariots are invisible and intangible, and it is hard to believe they are there.

We often depend first on one thing and then on another to advance our spiritual condition and to gain our spiritual victories. We "go down to Egypt for help" (Isaiah 31:1), and God is often obliged to destroy all our own earthly chariots before He can bring us to the point of climbing into His.

We lean too much upon a dear friend to help us progress in the spiritual life, and the Lord is obliged to separate us from that friend. We feel that all our spiritual prosperity depends on our continuance under the ministry of a favorite preacher, and he is mysteriously removed. We look upon our prayer meeting or our Bible class as the chief source of our spiritual strength, and we are prevented from attending them. And the "chariot of God" which alone can carry us to the places where we hoped to be taken by these things on which we have been depending, is to be found in the very deprivations we have mourned over. With the fire of His love, God must burn up every chariot of our own that stands in the way of our climbing into His.

We have to be brought to the place where things on which we depend fail us, before we can say, "He only." We say, "He *and*—something else," "He and my experience," "He and my church relationships," or "He and my Christian work." All that comes after the "and" must be taken away from us, or shown to be useless, before we can come to the "He only." As long as visible chariots are at hand the soul will not climb into the invisible ones.

Let us be thankful, then, for every trial that will help to destroy our earthly chariots and that will compel us to take refuge in the chariot of God which stands ready and waiting beside us in every event and circumstance of life. We are told that God "rideth upon the heavens" (Psalm 68:4), and if we want to ride with Him there, we need to be brought to the end of all riding upon the earth.

When we climb into God's chariot our goings are "established," for no obstacles can hinder His triumphal course. All losses, therefore, are gains that bring us to this. Paul understood this, and he gloried in the losses which brought him such unspeakable rewards. "But what things were gain to me, those I counted loss for Christ. Yea doubtless, and I count all things but loss for the excellency of the knowledge of Christ Jesus my Lord:

for whom I have suffered the loss of all things, and do count them but dung, that I may win Christ, and be found in Him" (Philippians 3:7-9).

Even the "thorn in the flesh" spoken of in 2 Corinthians 12:7, the messenger of Satan sent to buffet him, became a "chariot of God" to his willing soul. It carried him to the heights of triumph, which he could have reached in no other way. What is to "take pleasure" (2 Corinthians 12:10), but to turn them into the grandest of chariots?

Joseph had a revelation of his future triumphs and reigning, but the chariots that carried him there almost looked like vehicles of failure and defeat. Slavery and imprisonment are strange chariots to take one to a kingdom, and yet Joseph could have reached his exaltation by no other way. And our exaltation to the spiritual throne that awaits us is often reached by similar chariots.

Unseen Chariots

The great point, then, is to have our eyes opened to see everything that comes to us as a "chariot of God," and to learn how to climb into these chariots. We must recognize each thing that comes to us as being God's chariot for us and must accept it as from Him. Perhaps He doesn't command or originate the thing, but the moment we put it into His hands, it becomes His, and He at once turns it into a chariot for us. As it says in Romans 8:28, He makes "all things," even bad things, "work together for good to (all those who trust Him)". All He needs is to have it entirely committed to Him.

When your trial comes, put it right into the will of God and climb into that will as a little child climbs into its mother's arms. The baby carried in the chariot of its mother's arms rides triumphantly through the most difficult places and does not even know they are difficult. And how much more we ride triumphantly who are carried in the chariot of the "arms of God!"

Get into your chariot, then. Take each thing that is wrong in your lives as God's chariot for you. No matter who the builder of the wrong may be, whether men or devils, by the time it reaches your side it is God's chariot for you, meant to carry you to a heavenly place of triumph. Say, "Lord, open my eyes that I may see, not the visible enemy, but Thy unseen chariots of deliverance."

No doubt the enemy will try taunting you with the suggestion that God is not in your trouble and that there is no help for you in Him. But you must completely disregard all such suggestions and must overcome them with the assertion of a confident faith. "God is (my) refuge and strength, a very present help in time of trouble" (Psalm 46:1) must be your continual declaration, no matter what the causes may be.

Moreover, you must not be half-hearted about it. You must climb completely into your chariot, not with one foot dragging on the ground. There must be no "ifs" or "buts" or "supposings" or "questionings." You must accept God's will fully and must hide yourself in the arms of His love, always underneath to receive you, in every circumstance and at every moment. Say, "Thy will be done. Thy will be done," over and over. Shut out every other thought but the one thought of submitting to His will and trusting in His love. There can be no trials in which God's will does not have a place. The soul only has to climb into His will as in a chariot, and it will find itself "riding upon the heavens" with God, in a way it had never dreamed possible.

The soul that rides with God "on the sky" has views and sights of things that the soul which grovels on the earth can never have. The poor, crushed victim can only see the dust and stones and the grinding wheels, but the triumphant rider in the chariot sees far fairer sights.

You might ask where your chariots of God are to be found. The Psalmist says, "The chariots of God are twenty thousand, even thousands of angels" (Psalm 68:17). There is never a lack of chariots in any life. At the close of a meeting where I had been speaking about these chariots a dear Christian said to me, "I am a poor woman, and all my life have grieved that I could not drive a car like some of my rich neighbors. But I have been looking over my life while you have been talking, and I find that it is so full of chariots on every side that I am sure I will never need to walk again."

I don't have a shadow of doubt, dear readers, that if all our eyes could be opened today we would see our homes, our places of business, and the streets we travel filled with the "chariots of God." There is no need for any one of us to walk because of a lack of chariots. That irritating member of your household, who has, up to now, made life a burden to you and who has been trying to crush your soul into the dust, may from now on be a glorious chariot to carry you to the heights of heavenly patience and long-suffering. That misunderstanding, humiliation, unkindness, disappointment, loss, and defeat—all these are chariots waiting to carry you to the very heights of victory you have wanted to reach for so long.

Climb into them then, with thankful hearts, and lose sight of the causes of the trials in the shining of His love, which will "carry you in His arms" safely and triumphantly over it all.

Chapter 20

THE LIFE ON WINGS

This life hid with Christ in God has many aspects, and can be considered under a great many different figures. One aspect has been a great help and inspiration to me. I think it may also help some other longing and hungry souls. It is what I call the life on wings.

Our Lord has not only told us to consider the "lilies of the field" (Matthew 6:28), but also the "birds of the air" (Matthew 8:20). I have found that these little winged creatures have some wonderful lessons for us. In one of the Psalms, the Psalmist, after specifying the darkness and bitterness of his life in this earthly sphere of trial, cries out, "Oh that I had wings like a dove! for then would I fly away, and be at rest. Lo, then would I wander far off, and remain in the wilderness. I would hasten my escape from the windy storm and tempest" (Psalm 55:6-8).

This cry for "wings" is as old as humanity. Our souls were made to "mount up with wings." They can never be satisfied with anything short of flying.

The captive-born eagle feels within it the instinct of flight and is irritated and worried about its imprisonment, hardly knowing what it longs for. Our souls, too, are irritated and worried and cry out for freedom. We can never rest on earth, and we long to "fly away" from all that holds and hampers and imprisons us here.

In seeking an outward escape from our circumstances or from our miseries, restlessness and discontentment grow. At first we do not recognize that our only way of escape is to "mount up with wings" (Isaiah 40:31), and we try to "flee on horses," as the Israelites did, when oppressed by their trials (see Isaiah 30:16).

A Way Of Escape

Our "horses" are the outward things on which we depend for relief, some change of circumstance, or some help from man. We mount on these and run east or west, north or south—anywhere to get away from our trouble. In our ignorance we think that a change of our environment is all that is necessary to experience deliverance of our souls. But all such efforts to escape do not help. The soul is not made to "flee upon horses," but must make its flight always upon wings.

Moreover, as with the Israelites, these "horses" generally carry us out of one trouble only to land us in another. It is as the prophet Amos says, "As if a man did flee from a lion, and a bear met him; or went into the house, and leaned his hand on the wall, and a serpent bit him" (Amos 5:19).

How often have we also run from some "lion" in our pathway only to be met by a "bear." How often we have hidden ourselves in a place of supposed safety only to be bitten by a "serpent!" It is useless for the soul to hope to escape by running away from its troubles to any earthly refuge. There is not one that can give it deliverance.

Is there no way of escape for us, then, when in trouble or distress? Must we just plod wearily through it all and look for no relief? I rejoice to answer that there is a glorious way of escape for every one of us, if we will but mount up on wings and fly away from it all to God. It is not a way east or west or north or south, but it is a way upwards. "They that wait upon the Lord shall renew their strength; they shall mount up with wings as eagles; they shall run, and not be weary; and they shall walk, and not faint" (Isaiah 40:31).

All creatures that have wings can escape from every snare that is set from them, if only they will fly high enough. The soul that uses its wings can always find a sure "way to escape" from all that can hurt or trouble it.

What, then, are these wings? The secret is contained in the words, "They that wait upon the Lord." The soul that waits upon the Lord is the soul that is entirely surrendered to Him and trusts Him perfectly. Therefore, we might name our wings the wings of Surrender and of Trust. If we will only completely surrender ourselves to the Lord and trust Him perfectly, we will find our souls "mounting up with wings as eagles" to the "heavenly places" in Christ Jesus, where earthly annoyances or sorrows have no power to disturb us.

The wings of the soul carry it up into a spiritual plane of life, into the "life hid with Christ in God," which is a life utterly independent of circumstances, and one that no cage can imprison and no shackles bind.

The "things above" are the things the soul on wings cares about, not the "things on the earth." It views life and all its experiences from the high altitude of "heavenly places in Christ Jesus" (Ephesians 2:6). Things look very different according to the standpoint from which we view them. The caterpillar, as it creeps along the ground, must have a widely different "view" of the world around it, from that which the same caterpillar will have when its wings are developed, and it soars in the air above the very places where once it crawled. Similarly, the crawling soul must see things in a very different way from the soul that has "mounted up with wings." The mountain top may blaze with sunshine when the valley below is shrouded in fog. The bird whose wings can carry him high enough may mount at will out of the gloom below into the joy of the sunlight above.

Mount Up With Wings

Once, while spending a winter in London, I did not see any genuine sunshine for three long months because of the dense clouds of smoke that hung over the city like a shroud. But many times I saw that above the smoke the sun was shining. Once or twice through a rift I had a glimpse of a bird, with sunshine on its wings, sailing above the fog in the clear blue of the sunlit sky. Not all the brooms in London could sweep away the fog. But could we only mount high enough, we would reach a region above it all.

This is what the soul on wings does. It overcomes the world through faith. To overcome means to "come over" not to be crushed under, and the soul on wings flies over the world and the things of it. These lose their power to hold or bind the spirit that can "come over" them on the wings of Surrender and Trust. That spirit is made in very truth "more than conqueror" (Romans 8:37).

Birds overcome the lower law of gravitation by the higher law of flight. The soul on wings overcomes the lower law of sin and misery and bondage by the higher law of spiritual flying. The "law of the spirit of life in Christ Jesus" (Romans 8:2) must be a higher and more dominant law than the law of sin and death. Therefore, the soul that has mounted into this upper region of the life in Christ cannot fail to conquer and triumph.

But it may be asked how it is, then, that all Christians do not always triumph. I answer that it is because a great many Christians do not "mount up with wings" into this higher plane of life at all. They live on the same low level with their circumstances. Instead of flying over them, they try to fight them on their own earthly plane. On the earthly plane the soul is powerless. It has no weapons with which to conquer. Instead of overcoming (coming over) the trials and sorrows of the earthly life, it is overcome by them and crushed under them.

We all know, as I have said, that things look differently to us according to our "point of view." Trials assume a very different aspect when looked down upon from above, than when viewed from their own level. What seems like an impassable wall on its own level becomes an insignificant line to the eyes that see it from the top of a mountain. The snares and sorrows that assume such immense proportion while we look at them on the earthly plane, become insignificant when the soul has mounted on wings to the heavenly places above them.

A friend once illustrated the difference in her friends in the following way. She said, if all three came to a spiritual mountain which had to be crossed, the first one would tunnel through it with hard and wearisome labor. The second would meander around it in an indefinite fashion, hardly knowing where she was going, and yet, because her aim was right, would get around it at last. But the third, she said, would just flap her wings and fly right over. All of us must know something about this. If any of us in the past have tried to tunnel our way through the mountains that have stood across our pathway, or have been meandering around them, let us now resolve to spread our wings and "mount up" into the clear atmosphere

of God's presence. There it will be easy to overcome, or come over, the highest mountain of them
all.

Made For Heavenly Heights

I say, "spread our wings and mount up,"
because the largest wings ever known cannot lift a
bird one inch upward unless they are used. We
must *use* our wings, or they are of no help to us.

It is not worthwhile to say, "If I had wings I
would flee." For we already *have* the wings; we
should use them. The power to surrender and trust
exists in every human soul, and only needs to be
exercised. With these two wings we *can* "flee" to
God at any moment. But, in order really to reach
Him, we must actively use them. We must not
merely want to use them, we must *do* it definitely
and actively. A passive surrender or a passive trust
will not do. I mean this very practically. We will
not "mount up" very high, if we only surrender
and trust in theory, or in our especially spiritual
moments. We must do it definitely and practically,
about each detail of daily life as it comes to us.

We must meet our disappointments, our betray-
als, our persecutions, our malicious enemies, our
provoking friends, our trials and temptations of
every sort, with an active and experimental attitude of surrender and trust. We must spread our
wings and "mount up" to the "heavenly places in
Christ" above them all, where they will lose their
power to harm or distress us. For from these high
places we will see things through the eye of

Christ, and all earth will be glorified in the heavenly vision.

> "The dove has neither claw nor sting,
> Nor weapon for the fight;
> She owes her safety to the wing,
> Her victory to flight.
> The Bridegroom opens His arms of love,
> And in them folds the panting dove."

How changed our lives would be if we could only fly through the days on these wings of surrender and trust! Instead of stirring up strife and bitterness by trying to fight offending brothers and sisters, we should escape all strife by simply spreading our wings and mounting up to the heavenly region. There our eyes would see all things covered with a mantle of Christian love and pity.

Our souls were made to live in this upper atmosphere, and we stifle and choke on any lower level. Our eyes were made to look off from these heavenly heights, and our vision is distorted by any lower gazing. It is a great blessing, therefore, that our loving Father in heaven has mercifully arranged all the discipline of our lives with a view to teaching us to fly.

In Deuteronomy we have a picture of how this teaching is done: "As an eagle stirreth up her nest, fluttereth over her young, spreadeth abroad her wings, taketh them, beareth them on her wing: so the Lord alone did lead him, and there was no strange god with him" (Deuteronomy 32:11-12).

The mother eagle teaches her little ones to fly by

making their nest so uncomfortable that they are forced to leave it and commit themselves to the unknown world of air outside. God does the same to us. He stirs up our comfortable nests, pushes us over the edge of them, and we are forced to use our wings to save ourselves from fatal falling. Read your trials in this light, and see if you cannot begin to get a glimpse of their meaning. Your wings are being developed.

I knew a lady whose life was one long strain of trial, from a cruel, wicked, drunken husband. There was no possibility of human help, and in her despair she was driven to use her wings and fly to God. And during the long year of trial her wings grew so strong from constant flying, that at last, when the trials were at their hardest, it seemed to her as if her soul was carried over them on a beautiful rainbow and found itself in a peaceful resting place on the other side.

Hindrances To Flying

With this end in view we can surely accept with thankfulness every trial that compels us to use our wings, for only then can they grow strong and large and fit for the highest flying. Unused wings gradually wither and shrink and lose their flying power. If we had nothing in our lives that made flying necessary, we might at last lose all capacity to fly.

But you may ask, "Are there no hindrances to flying, even where the wings are strong, and the soul is trying hard to use them?" I answer, "Yes."

A bird may be imprisoned in a cage; it may be tethered to the ground with a cord; it may be loaded with a weight that drags it down, or it may be entrapped in the "snare of the fowler" (Psalm 91:3). Hindrances may make it impossible for the soul to fly, until it has been set free from them by the mighty power of God.

One "snare of the fowler" that entraps many souls is the snare of doubt. The doubts look so plausible and often so humble, that Christians walk into their "snare" without dreaming for a moment that it is a snare at all, until they find themselves caught and unable to fly. There is no more possibility of flying for the soul that doubts, than there is for the bird caught in the fowler's snare.

The reason for this is evident. One of our wings, namely, the wing of trust, is entirely disabled by the slightest doubt. Just as it requires two wings to lift a bird in the air, it requires two wings to lift the soul. A great many people do everything but trust. They spread the wing of surrender, and use it vigorously. They wonder why they do not mount up, never dreaming that it is because all the while the wing of trust is hanging idle by their sides. It is because Christians use only one wing, that their efforts to fly are often so irregular and fruitless.

Look at a bird with a broken wing trying to fly, and you will get some idea of the kind of motion all one-sided flying must make. We must use both our wings, or not try to fly at all.

It may be that for some the "snare of the fowler" is some subtle form of sin, some hidden want of consecration. Where this is the case, the wing of trust may seem to be all right, but the wing of surrender hangs idly down. It is just as hopeless to try to fly with the wing of trust alone, as with the wing of surrender alone. Both wings must be used, or no flying is possible.

Or perhaps the soul may feel as if it were in a prison from which it cannot escape, and consequently is unable to mount up on wings. No earthly bars can ever imprison the soul. No walls however high, or bolts however strong, can imprison an eagle, so long as there is an open way upward. Earth's power can never hold the soul in prison while the upward way is kept open and free. Our enemies may build walls around us as high as they please, but they cannot build any barrier between us and God. If we "mount up with wings," we can fly higher than any of their walls can ever reach.

If we find ourselves imprisoned, we may be sure that it is not our earthly environment that constitutes our jail cell, for the soul's wings scorn all petty bars and walls of earth's making. The only thing that can really imprison the soul is something that hinders its upward flight. Isaiah 59:2 tells us "your iniquities have separated between you and your God, and your sins have hid His face from you, that He will not hear." Therefore, if our soul is imprisoned, it must be because some indulged sin has built a barrier between us and the Lord, and we cannot fly until this sin is given up and put out of the way.

Cut Loose From Earthly Ties

But often, where there is no conscious sin, the soul is still unconsciously tethered to something of earth. It struggles in vain to fly. Some of my friends once got into a boat in Norway to row around one of the inlets there. They took their seats and began to row vigorously, but the boat made no headway. They put out more strength and rowed harder than before, but all in vain. The boat didn't move an inch. Then someone remembered that the boat had not been unmoored, and he exclaimed, "No wonder we could not get away, when we were trying to pull the whole continent of Europe after us!" Our souls are likewise often not unmoored from earthly things. We must cut ourselves loose. As an eagle might try to fly with a hundred-ton weight tied fast to its feet, the soul may try to "mount up with wings" while a weight of earthly cares and anxieties is holding it down to earth.

When our Lord was trying to teach His disciples concerning this danger, He told them a parable of a great supper to which many who were invited failed to come because they were hindered by their earthly cares. One had bought a piece of land, another a yoke of oxen, and a third had married a wife. They felt that all these things needed their care.

Wives or oxen or land or even smaller things may be the cords that tether the soul from flying or the weight that holds it down. Let us then cut every cord and remove every barrier so our souls may find no hindrance to their mounting up with wings as eagles to heavenly places in Christ Jesus.

We are commanded to have our hearts filled with songs of rejoicing and to make inward melody to the Lord. But unless we mount up with wings this is impossible, for the only creature that can sing is the creature that flies. Though all the world should be desolate, Habakkuk 3:18 says, "Yet I will rejoice in the Lord, I will joy in the God of my salvation." Paul knew what it was to use his wings when he found himself "sorrowful, yet always rejoicing" (2 Corinthians 6:10). On the earthly plane all was dark to both, but on the heavenly plane all was brightest sunshine.

Do you know anything about this life on wings? Do you "mount up" continually to God, out of and above earth's cares and trials, to that higher plane of life where all is peace and triumph? Or, do you plod wearily along on foot through the midst of your trials and let them overwhelm you at every turn?

Let us guard against a mistake here. Do not think that by flying I mean very joyous emotions or feelings of exhilaration. There is a great deal of emotional flying that is not really flying at all. It is such flying as a feather accomplishes which is driven upward by a strong puff of wind, but flutters down again as soon as the wind ceases to blow. The flying I mean is a matter of *principle,* not a matter of *emotion*. It may be accompanied by very joyous emotions, but it does not depend on them. It depends only upon the facts of an entire surrender and an absolute trust. Everyone who will honestly use these two wings and will faithfully persist in using them will find that they *have* mounted up with wings as an eagle, no matter how empty of all emotion they may have felt themselves to be before.

For the promise is sure: "They that wait upon the Lord shall mount up with wings as eagles." Not "may perhaps mount up," but *"shall."* It is the inevitable result. May we each one prove it for ourselves!